BROMELIADS

for the contemporary garden

BROMELIADS

for the contemporary garden

Andrew Steens

Timber Press
Portland • Cambridge

Acknowledgements

This book is dedicated to my mother, Clasina Steens, who inspired my love of plants, and to the memory of my father, Theodorus Steens, who was in no way a gardener, but instilled in me many other essential life values.

I could not have completed the book without the patience and support of my extended family, in particular my partner Angela Wain and her mother Glenda, who looked after the home front, including my newborn son Theo and his sister Katelyn. Douglas Crosbie, who looks after my bromeliads and my sister Mandy, who helped keep us afloat. Glenda also provided several lovely photos, as did my sister Dorothy.

In writing this book, I have had the assistance of many keen gardeners who have opened their gardens for photographing. In particular, I would like to thank Steve and Linda Durrant of Whenuapai, Peter Brady of Mt Eden, Alex Schanzer Landscaping of Pukekohe, P. & S. Mrsich of Podgora gardens in Waipu, Robin Booth of Wharepuke Gardens in Kerikeri, Jenny Daniels of Whangaparoa, and the Austen brothers of Exotic Nurseries in Kaitaia.

Thanks also to Jane Connor of Timber Press (USA) and Peter Arthur of Touchwood Books, for getting me started, Tom Beran of Random House New Zealand for keeping me going, and Sarah Elworthy and the team for their patience in getting the book right.

Finally, a special thanks to Peter Waters, scientific officer for the Bromeliad Society of New Zealand and a director of the Bromeliad Society International, for carefully checking names and descriptions of the bromeliads in this book.

First published in North America in 2003 by
Timber Press, Inc.
The Haseltine Building
133 S.W. Second Avenue, Suite 450
Portland, Oregon 97204, USA
tel 1-800-327-5680 or 1-503-227-2878
fax 1-503-227-3070
www.timberpress.com

and distributed in the United Kingdom by
Timber Press
2 Station Road
Swavesy, Cambridge CB4 5QJ
tel (01954) 232959
fax (01954) 206040

ISBN 0-88192-604-3

A CIP record for this book is available from the Library of Congress and the British Library

Front cover photograph: *Vriesea hieroglyphica*; back cover photographs (top to bottom): *Neoregelia* hybrid, *Neoregelia* 'Lamberts Pride', *Vriesea carinata*, *Vriesea philippo-coburgii*.

Book design and production: Sarah Elworthy

Printed in China

CONTENTS

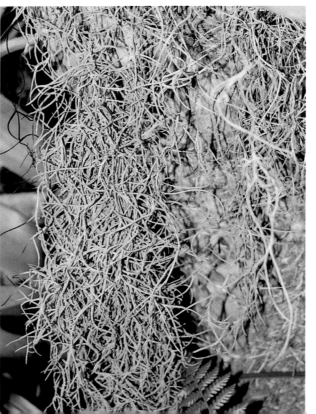

INTRODUCTION

Bromeliads used to be one of the best-kept secrets in the plant kingdom. Native to the American continents, from eastern Virginia in the United States to the tip of Argentina, these magnificent plants have only recently become widespread in gardens around the world. As the new millennium begins, they are taking their rightful place as some of the most popular plants for gardeners in temperate, subtropical and tropical regions.

Although many bromeliad species, cultivars and hybrids are described in this book, it is not a comprehensive listing of species for their own sake, or a description of the latest and most fantastic hybrids. Some of the larger genera, such as *Tillandsia* and *Guzmania*, are touched on only lightly; they are fantastic plants in their own right, but are not as useful for most gardens as other genera such as *Aechmea*, *Neoregelia* and *Nidularium*. Instead the focus is on plants that will do well in most gardens, and more importantly, I have tried to describe those plants most commonly available. Nothing is more frustrating than trying to find a fabulous bromeliad you have seen in an article or a book, not realising that it may be a new species or hybrid with less than 1000 plants in cultivation worldwide.

Similarly, although every care has been taken with plant names and descriptions, it is difficult to ensure complete accuracy, given the many thousands of hybrids and the frequency with which botanists make changes to specific names and even generic names. The arguments between botanists over nomenclature are endless and often very complex. It is not an area I will go into, as this book is intended simply for the home gardener who wishes to successfully grow these amazing and beautiful plants.

This book is written by a gardener, for gardeners, who I hope will come to love these plants as much as I do.

Opposite, top: A lush landscape featuring many different bromeliads. Bottom left: *Neoregelia* 'Kings Ransom' is a rare and sought-after cultivar of *Neoregelia carolinae*. Bottom right: Twisted strands of *Tillandsia usneoides*.

THE BROMELIAD FAMILY

The Bromeliad family comprises nearly 3000 species at the time of writing, contained in 56 genera. New species are constantly being found, in fact up to four new species are described every month. No doubt there are still many more to be discovered, as bromeliads are expert at filling every nook and cranny available in the vast South American continent and the lower North American continent. Only one known species comes from another continent, *Pitcairnia feliciana*, from western Africa, and it is possible this plant spread via birds or ocean drift; however, it may also indicate the origins of the family some 66 million years ago (the oldest fossil record dates back some 30 million years) before the continents of Africa and South America drifted apart.

Most bromeliads grow as a rosette of leaves, usually without any stem, although there are exceptions to this as there are to any generalisation regarding these plants. Experienced collectors are never surprised to find a new bromeliad that defies all previous growth habits. For example, several tillandsias form long stems over time and a few of the neoregelias can form a short stem on aged plants. There are even a few *Tillandsia* species that form a true bulb, albeit an aerial one.

The size of the plants varies considerably. The smallest, *Tillandsia usneoides*, is usually less than 3 cm in diameter, while the largest, *Puya raimondii*, can grow more than 10 m tall when in flower.

The foliage takes many different shapes, from needle thin to broad and flat, symmetrical to bizarre, soft to spiky. These different forms have developed in response to each species' native habitat and understanding these environmental influences can help the gardener considerably when planting bromeliads.

Bromeliads provide the most amazing collection of foliage colours and patterns found in the plant world. Foliage colours range from gold, through various shades of green, to deep maroon, with many colours in between.

Many bromeliads have variegated leaves, with white, cream, yellow and even red variegations. Some are banded with silver, maroon or black. Others are spotted with red, cream or purple. Quite a few have a different colour on the underside of the leaf to the top.

In addition to the foliage, many bromeliads have dazzling and sometimes bizarre flower clusters or spikes. The most showy are truly magnificent, while the smallest flowers measure only 2–3 mm across. Even these tiny flowers can be quite amazing, with incredible detail and lustrous beauty rarely seen in other flowers.

The range of flower types in this diverse and fascinating group of plants is considerably more than in any other plant family. Some are borne on huge spikes which reach over 10 m tall; in others the upright spike may measure only several centimetres. The upright stalks may be branched or simple. The flower spikes can retain their colours for as little as a couple of weeks, to as much as 12 months, depending on the species.

In some species the flower stalk is virtually nonexistent, with the flowers appearing deep in the vase of the plants. Sometimes the flowers are virtually unseen, with all the beauty of flowering concentrated on the changing colours of the foliage.

Many bromeliads have hanging flower spikes, where the tip of the inflorescence can actually hang down lower than the plant itself.

Some bromeliad flowers are faintly scented, with several that are heavily perfumed. The scents are quite unlike most flowering plants; for example, *Tillandsia cyanea* smells exactly like the clove spice, and can be quite strong when several plants are in flower.

BROMELIAD HISTORY

Humans began using bromeliads for food, protection, fibre and ceremonial use several thousand years ago. The early civilisations of the Inca, Aztec, Maya and others all used bromeliads extensively, and even today their descendants continue to use them for the same purposes. Each Christmas, thousands of tillandsias are harvested for nativity scenes, the small ones to imitate snow or the flowers of larger species to provide decoration.

European interest in the Bromeliad family was initially focused on the pineapple, *Ananas comosus*, which the Spanish conquistadors quickly realised was a fruit fit for kings. It was introduced into Europe approximately 500 years ago and quickly became a sensation, although at that time only the wealthiest could afford to build the heated greenhouses needed to house these exotic plants. Even today, the impact the introduction of this fruit had can be seen in the stone and marble representations of the pineapple adorning many old English and European gardens.

The next bromeliad to 'arrive' in Europe was *Guzmania lingulata* var. *minor* in 1776, which caused a major sensation among wealthy gardeners. In 1828 *Aechmea fasciata* was introduced, followed by *Vriesea splendens* in 1840. It is fascinating to note, as well as a testament to their dazzling beauty, that all three of these plants are still among the most widely grown bromeliads worldwide.

By the late 1800s breeders in Belgium, France and the Netherlands had begun hybridising plants for the wholesale trade. Many great vriesea hybrids in particular, were produced over the next decades, but the First World War halted a large number of the breeding programmes and many good hybrids were lost. Bromeliads did not experience a resurgence in popularity until after the Second World War.

Below: The large flowers of *Tillandsia cyanea* have a lovely scent of cloves.

Since the early 1950s, mainly Dutch, but also Belgian and North American nurseries have expanded bromeliad production hugely. Now bromeliads are grown and sold in their millions throughout Europe and the United States — more than 20 million flowering plants are sold each year through the Dutch auction system alone.

In the late 1970s *Tillandsia* became fashionable, sold to the general public as 'air plants' and typically glued to pieces of rock, driftwood, crystal or ornaments. But by the 1990s they had come to be seen as tacky, and unfortunately many millions of *Tillandsia* were killed through neglect, largely due to the misconceptions that developed from the use of the term 'air plant'. However, many current bromeliad fanciers started with one of these plants.

In the 21st century bromeliads, including *Tillandsia*, are at the peak of garden fashion. Leading landscapers are using them in nearly every design, and all over the world, gardeners are realising that bromeliads add the finishing touch to the modern landscape. Bromeliads are becoming one of the most sought-after plants for modern interiors and offices, apartment balconies and suburban gardens,

Top left: It is hardly surprising that *Guzmania lingulata* var. *minor* caused such a flurry of interest when it was first discovered. Top right: The urn plant, *Aechmea fasciata* has been grown as an indoor plant for centuries.
Above: Tens of thousands of *Vriesea* 'Poelmanii White Line' plants in a Dutch glasshouse.

and societies and clubs dedicated to these plants are springing up everywhere. The trend is not confined to tropical and subtropical regions like Hawaii or Queensland, but extends to colder areas such as southern England, Portugal, southern Texas and northern California, due to the growing awareness of the many cold-hardy members of the Bromeliad family.

WHAT ARE BROMELIADS?

Bromeliads are some of the more recent plants to evolve; consequently, they are still rapidly evolving and are very diverse and highly adapted to filling niches in the environment that other plants have not yet taken advantage of.

In their native habitats bromeliads grow in altitudes from sea level to as high as 4200 m, and in varied terrain from rainforests to deserts. Approximately half the species are true air plants or epiphytes which grow on trees or other plants, deriving their nutrients from rainfall, dust and debris collecting in their cupped shape, or absorbing them through special scales on their leaves. Some species are saxicolous, which means that they grow over rocks; others are terrestrial, using the soil for support and sustenance.

Nearly all bromeliads have specialised groups of cells called trichomes, which form scales. In each group these scales are slightly different in shape and function. In most bromeliads the scales serve mainly as a very efficient absorption system for water and nutrients. However, they can also serve as protection from dry conditions or from the cold, as a rain protection system (essential in some of the wet tropical areas), as an anti-fouling system to stop the leaves from getting clogged with dirt; they also provide protection from fungal and insect attack and excess UV rays. They are one of the main reasons why bromeliads are so successful in filling so many niches in the ecosystem.

The xerophytic (atmospheric) epiphytes have so many of these trichomes that the plants appear grey or silver; their multitudinous scales help to reduce water loss and shield them from solar radiation. These xerophytic epiphytes survive off the moisture and nutrients in the atmosphere alone and will not grow in soil or potting mix

Above: *Tillandsia* roots mould to the shape of the driftwood, clinging on fiercely.

— they need to be attached to a branch, rock or similar structure. The few roots that they produce are typically very hard, wiry and incapable of taking up water or nutrients, and are called holdfast roots, as they serve only to fasten the plant to the host.

Some people consider epiphytic bromeliads to be parasites, but this is not so as they do not feed off the tree they are attached to. The host tree is simply a perch the bromeliad uses to get into a more favourable position for light — indeed it is not uncommon for objects like telephone wires and fences to be covered in species of *Tillandsia*, sometimes in such numbers that their weight breaks the wires.

Many of the non-xerophytic, but still epiphytic, bromeliads however, can be adapted to grow in or on soil. This is a useful adaptation, for if the bromeliad falls off the tree it may be able to continue growing if it lands in the right spot. Alternatively, if humus builds up around the base of the plant while in a perch the root system can make full use of it, and then the structure of the root system actually changes. The holdfast roots no longer appear, instead much softer roots are produced, which are covered in fine root hairs much like normal plants. These can take up water and nutrients from the surrounding leaf mould or soil.

Many epiphytic and some terrestrial bromeliads have specially constructed leaf rosettes capable of holding water in the centre and are known as tank bromeliads. They are also able to take water and nutrients through the trichomes found in large numbers at the base of the leaves, but rely heavily on the storage of water and nutrients in the centre to keep them going during unfavourable months. The terrestrial types will also take in water and nutrients through the roots, giving them more flexibility in different environmental conditions.

The saxicolous bromeliads, which use their root systems partly for support, are often found clinging precariously to cliff faces. However, their roots can also take up nutrients and water if they happen upon a pocket of soil or debris.

The group of bromeliads known as terrestrials use their roots in the same way other plants do, and their root system is also well developed in contrast to most other bromeliads. Except for the terrestrial tank bromeliads, they do not hold water in their rosette, and usually rely on the availability of water and nutrients in the surrounding soil. The leaf trichomes are still present on these plants, but as they are usually non-absorbent or are of much less importance for taking up water and nutrients. However, the trichomes may still be essential for survival, as they sometimes cover the plants so thickly that a frost barrier is formed, as seen in *Puya laxa* and others.

BROMELIADS IN THEIR NATURAL ENVIRONMENT

A quick tour of some of the native habitats of bromeliads can give many clues as to their suitability in the garden. They live naturally in many different ecosystems across the vast South American continent, Central America and the lower North American continent, where they form an essential part of the environment, often providing the only source of water during the dry season. By looking at the following selection of habitats one can gain a better understanding of bromeliads and their use in the garden.

Often the first habitat that springs to mind when thinking of bromeliads is the vast Amazon River basin. The Amazon River itself is some 6000 km long, and contains a number of ecosystems along its length, but the main one is the huge jungle basin which consists of impenetrable vegetation of the lushest kind. The lushness is a result of the near-constant, even temperatures all year round, high rainfall and humidity, and the speed at which essential nutrients are recycled and reused. However, despite the popular belief that most bromeliads come from the Amazon, this region actually has less endemic species than many other areas; not only that, but many Amazon species are unsuited to gardens in the temperate and subtropical regions, unless grown in greenhouses.

Another well-known habitat is the tropical rainforests of Guyana and Venezuela, which cover vast areas of both countries (almost 80 percent of Guyana is rainforest). These forests have many different ecosystems and a rich biodiversity, and have many sheer-sided rock formations, commonly called tabletop mountains and locally called 'tepui'. Many are completely inaccessible except by helicopter. These forests and flood plains are home to many beautiful and some bizarre bromeliads, including the

Below: *Tillandsia bulbosa* mounted on a small piece of driftwood.

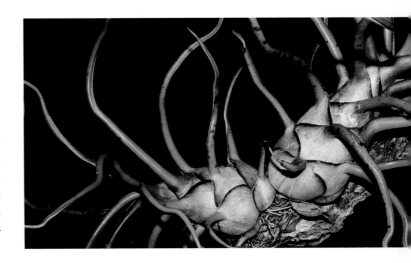

rare and primitive but gorgeous navias. Bromeliads cover every surface, including sand-banks along the riversides, rocky cliffs and they even live in the spray zone of the waterfalls.

Another native habitat for many epiphytic bromeliads is the montane cloud forests in the mountains of Cerro Jefe, in the Republic of Panama. Typical of many of the cloud forest habitats which bromeliads enjoy throughout Central and South America, rainfall is very high, up to 4 m per year, and some aerial moisture in the form of either mist or rain occurs nearly every day. Temperatures in these cloud forests tend to be cooler than the surrounding tropical lowlands, usually temperatures do not move beyond the range of 15–30°C. Despite the near-constant rain and cloud, light levels are reasonably high due to the altitude, so bromeliad growth is prolific.

Because of these temperatures, many of the species from the cloud forests of Cerro Jefe will grow quite well in subtropical or the warmer temperate gardens; however, most will suffer if temperatures drop below 5°C, which limits their use in cooler gardens. Some of the more notable bromeliads from this region are *Aechmea allenii*, *A. dactylina*, *Guzmania desautelsii*, *G. lingulata*, *G. musaica* and *Tillandsia bulbosa*.

It is widely believed that the Bromeliad family arose in the Andean highlands of South America, as this is where the greatest concentration of primitive members of this family reside. Even now, many species are endemic to the Andean highlands, from northern Chile to Colombia. There are two main zones in this region, the moist mountain forests of the lower slopes, between 1500–2500 m above sea level, and the high, cold, dry plateaus and mountain sides of the upper Andes. In the moist mountain forests, conditions are best described as warm temperate for the most part; moist air is present for several hours each day in the form of clouds or mist and rainfall tends to be quite regular.

Dry desert-like conditions prevail in many parts of the South American and lower North American continents. Some of these areas are formed by coastal conditions, such as the vast Peruvian coastal deserts where bromeliads such as *Tillandsia straminea*, *T. purpurea* and *T. latifolia* grow

in great drifts on the sand, making dunes form behind them.

Another large and important bromeliad area are the tropical dry zones of Mexico, such as southern Puebla, where xerophytic and tank-forming epiphytes abound. *Tillandsia* species are often found growing on the trunk of cacti, particularly the tall *Cephalocereus* species. The other genus commonly found in this area is *Hechtia* which form great colonies of large rosettes over the dry limestone rocks. At the upper altitudes of these tropical dry regions extensive oak forests are found, draped with tresses of *Tillandsia usneoides* and many other *Tillandsia* and *Vriesea* species. Incongruously to gardeners from the cooler climates, the oak forests often have palm trees growing among them.

The Chaco region of northern Argentina is a similar dry tropical habitat, where the large terrestrial *Aechmea* such as *A. distichantha* and imposing, heavily spined *Bromelia* species are often found among scattered stands of silk floss trees (*Chorisia* spp).

The Atlantic coastal forests and scrub of south-eastern and southern Brazil from Rio de Janeiro to Rio Grande do Sul state are very important habitats for bromeliads.

Below: Some of the *Hechtia* genus have beautiful markings on their leaves.

Relatively high temperatures all year round, coupled with even rainfall and quite fertile soil, make this a lush region, originally covered by tropical rainforest but now largely cleared for development and farming. Those remnants give some indication of how it must have been before the deforestation. In parts, bromeliads cover almost every available surface including the ground, where many of the *Nidularium* genus can be found. On the ground, but more often in trees are many *Vriesea* species, including *V. incurvata* and *V. philippo-coburgii*. Near the sea itself, hardy species such as *Dyckia encholirioides* and *D. maritima* can be found on rocks and tall near-vertical cliffs, immediately adjacent to the water.

Dry scrub and grasslands comprise most of the north-eastern Brazilian state of Goiás, where drought-tolerant plants such as *Aechmea bromeliifolia, Dyckia marnier-lapostollei, D. brasiliana* and *Tillandsia didisticha* abound. Drought tolerance is much needed here, as this region is almost totally arid for the five months from May to September.

Although most bromeliads come from Central and South America, some species are native to North America. In mainland United States, there are several areas with large and important bromeliad populations. The most notable is south Florida, in the vast swamps and hammocks of the Everglades region, where approximately 16 species are found. Here warm and humid conditions prevail for most of the year, but bromeliad growth is limited at the northern edge by periodically severe frosts. Some of Florida's more stunning and interesting bromeliads include *Guzmania monostachia, Tillandsia fasciculata, T. variabilis* and *T. utriculata*.

Bromeliads themselves provide a habitat for many thousands of species of other plants, as well as reptiles, amphibians, crustaceans, insects and other creatures. Sometimes, the relationship is so close that certain animals are found only where there are bromeliads, an extreme example being the endangered golden Coqui frog of Puerto Rico, which is found only where there is a density of bromeliad tanks exceeding one plant per metre. Similarly, some carnivorous plants, such as several species of bladderwort, are found only with bromeliads.

An astonishing symbiotic relationship is found on the island of Jamaica, where the bromeliad crab (*Metopaulias depressus*) is found almost exclusively in the vases and leaf bases of *Aechmea paniculigera*, all year round. Unlike other crabs, where it is literally 'crab eat crab', this species has evolved in the bromeliad habitat to such an extent that the crabs develop in colonies of a queen mother crab and her offspring. The relationship is often symbiotic, with the plant supplying water and shelter, and the other organism providing protection or nutrients. This is the case with some of the bulb-forming species of *Tillandsia*, such as *T. caput medusae* and *T. butzii*, where the closed cavities of the leaf sheaths that form the bulb become home to ants which both protect the plants from herbivores and provide nutrients from waste products.

Outside bromeliads' natural habitats and in the garden, many similar relationships will form in any country they inhabit. In New Zealand it is reasonably common to find the giant weta sheltering in bromeliads. The Australian golden bell frog loves the environment created by bromeliads and, of course, spiders anywhere thrive in them.

In their natural habitat, sometimes even in National Parks, many bromeliads are threatened or have become extinct through thoughtless habitat destruction and activities like commercial harvesting, logging, mining or clearance for farming. As South and Central American countries expand their populations, urban sprawl consumes increasingly large areas. The urban sprawl has negative side effects such as the recent destruction of hundreds of large *Alcantarea imperialis* which grow on the bare granite slopes in the mountains around the city of Rio de Janeiro in a misguided attempt to control disease-carrying mosquitoes. Species such as *Tillandsia argentea, T. butzii* and *T. ionantha* are now heavily protected and are not legally allowed to be collected, with most plants now raised by commercial growers to meet market demand.

However, there are also many bromeliad species now extinct in the wild that are commonly available as garden plants, saved through the efforts of collectors and nurseries.

LANDSCAPING WITH BROMELIADS

Landscaping with bromeliads in tropical and subtropical gardens is very simple, with just a few basic rules. Bromeliads are some of the toughest plants in existence, proving very adaptable to a wide range of conditions. However, there is a big difference between a bromeliad grown to its maximum potential and one that is just surviving. The key to successful gardening with bromeliads is the same as for successful real estate trading: 'location, location, location'. Fortunately, there is a location for every bromeliad and a bromeliad for every location. Gardeners in temperate climates should consult the information on pot culture, greenhouses, and cold-hardiness in the following pages for choices available to them.

IN SHADY GARDENS

Many gardens, particularly older gardens, are quite shady. As gardens mature, shade levels increase, even where planting has been well planned. Use bromeliads wherever bright colours and dramatic foliage are needed in shady gardens: beside trickling streams, along mossy paths, surrounding quiet pools and under subtropical foliage.

Established gardens, especially those with patches of dense native forest creating dappled light, are ideal for bromeliads that are adapted to shade — in their native environment these can be found on or near the forest floor. Some direct sunlight can be tolerated, but only in the early morning or very late afternoon; most of these plants will either scorch or lose leaf colour with more sun than this.

This page, below: *Vriesea hieroglyphica* and *Asplenium nidus* make a striking combination.

Opposite, top left: A well-established clump of *Nidularium fulgens* on this old tree fern stump makes a nice display.
Top right: Rich burgundy and glossy green make a lovely contrast on *Aechmea* 'Royal Wine'.
Bottom: Soft-leaved bromeliads planted with ferns in a shady subtropical glade.

With some thought, stunning effects can be created with these plants.

Shady spots in the garden are ideal for quiet contemplation on a hot summer's day. Plan your bromeliad planting to allow the mind to focus on shapes and patterns. A quiet dell planted with soft ferns and mosses is no longer ordinary when the mottled foliage of *Nidularium fulgens* is included. Over winter, when a lift in spirits may be needed, this plant will oblige with brilliant red star-shaped flowerheads.

Many of the shade-loving bromeliads have wine-red or burgundy foliage, particularly on the underside of the leaves. This is a natural adaptation for the shade, as this warm colour acts as an internal reflector of light, allowing the plants to capture as much as they can. The bonus for the gardener is that this adaptation also makes for beautiful plants. Use these where a subtle colour lift is needed in the garden. *Aechmea* hybrids such as A. 'Big Stuff', 'Black Jack', 'Fosters Favorite', 'Red Wine' and 'Royal Wine' all look very sleek and glossy in the shade. All of these plants have pendulous flowerheads consisting of vibrant berry-like flowers which can last for months. A useful trick is to plant these in a swathe, with high points created by planting some over tree fern stumps. This allows garden visitors a view of the deep underside colour and shows off the hanging flower spikes to their best.

Another stunning burgundy-coloured bromeliad for deep shade is *Canistropsis billbergioides* 'Plum', which has a star-shaped flowerhead in the same colour as the foliage. These small but remarkable plants will look fabulous arising from a bed of soft green Baby's tears (*Soleirolia soleirolii*).

Variegated bromeliads are something quite special and no other family of plants produces variegated species as readily as bromeliads. Many of these are long established and justifiably famous. *Neoregelia carolinae* 'Tricolor' was

Top left: *Neoregelia carolinae* hybrids surround a mosaic pool.
Middle: The bold stripes of *Nidularium innocentii lineatum* make it the centrepiece of this shady garden.
Left: A dense stand of *Aechmea gamosepala* after only three years of growth.

one of the first variegated bromeliads to be introduced to gardeners and is still one of the favourites with its striking rosettes of green with ivory stripes, overlaid with a blush of pink. When flowering the central leaves turn vibrant crimson. No garden can fail to be eye-catching with a bed of these plants glowing out from the shade. There have been many hybrids produced from this plant, all with varying degrees of variegation and leaf colour but all of them equally dazzling.

The variegated neoregelias are some of the best bromeliads for planting under deciduous trees. They adapt to the changing light levels faster than many others, as they respond to increasing light by increasing the amount of pink tinge over the green and white portions of the leaves.

Other neoregelias also adapt well to shady areas, and there is nothing like the intensity of a flowering *N. carolinae* hybrid to bring life to a shady corner. This is one of the most hybridised species in the Bromeliad family and they come in many colours, from soft pink through all the shades of red and cerise, with even purple and mauve varieties available. With such a range of colours, gardeners can mix and match to suit their taste. Contrast colours against the vibrancy of vireyas, for example, or blend sublimely with similar shades.

Neoregelias are also ideal for dry shady areas, common in gardens with large mature trees, particularly conifers or eucalypts. Many plants struggle in the combination of shade and drought; however, the tough neoregelias with their custom-made water reservoirs and drought-resistant foliage can easily cope with just a light watering every few weeks or so.

Some of the *Aechmea* genus have lovely glossy green foliage which always gives a tropical feel to any shady garden. These green-leaved aechmeas are often very fast growers so are ideal for carpeting large areas quickly. One of the best groundcovers for shady areas is *A. gamosepala* along with its many hybrids; single plants may spread to cover a square metre in the space of two or three years, choking out most weeds in the process. In autumn, the brightly coloured flower spikes liberally cover the bed.

Another beautiful plant for the shade is the green-leaved

Above: *Canistropsis billbergioides* 'Persimmon' is one of the best plants for deep shade.

Aechmea weilbachii, which can become quite stately over time. A clump of these among mossy rocks can be quite a conversation piece, particularly when the tall flower spikes of vibrant berries arise.

The real stars of the shady garden though are the nidulariums. Nearly all of this genus is adapted for full shade, although some dappled light is beneficial. Their flat but perfectly formed rosettes with their classic star-shaped flowers are very well behaved, and therefore ideal for smaller gardens like apartment courtyards, where the sun may never reach. Ideal over rounded rocks or pebbles, they are also very low-maintenance. Their shape also lends itself to surrounding small formal water features. Some, such as N. 'Madame Robert Morobe' can grow quite large, at over half a metre across.

The colour of the star-shaped flower bracts can last for up to six months and come in a variety of hues, from the shocking pink of N. 'Lila Rosea' to the deep red of *N. rutilans* and the amazing blue of *N. antoineanum*.

Where a natural-looking pond is being planned, consider turning it into a jungle pool. Casually toss a piece of driftwood or tree fern log over one edge of the pond and

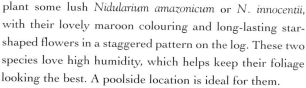

Above: An Australian Golden Bell frog sheltering in a *Vriesea hieroglyphica*. Right: A *Vriesea* 'Intermedia' hybrid looks stunning in this dark subtropical garden.

plant some lush *Nidularium amazonicum* or *N. innocentii*, with their lovely maroon colouring and long-lasting star-shaped flowers in a staggered pattern on the log. These two species love high humidity, which helps keep their foliage looking the best. A poolside location is ideal for them.

On the shadiest reaches of the pond, use some *Canistropsis billbergioides* to sprawl their lush green foliage over the edge and draw the eye with their orange, yellow or red stars. Strategically place a couple of dramatic *Vriesea hieroglyphica* to one side among a bed of maidenhair ferns or soft mosses. On the lower side of the pool, the grassy foliage of the moisture-loving *Pitcairnia flammea* and *P. xanthocalyx* will absorb any overflow. Don't be surprised if your pond and the surrounding bromeliads become home to frogs, as bromeliads are a natural habitat for these amphibians.

The *Vriesea* genus also has many members well adapted to shady gardens, and their bright spear-shaped flower spikes ensure plenty of colour all year round. Although a number of the smaller shade-loving vrieseas are quite tender, there are some reasonably hardy ones that can be

used with confidence in a shaded garden, where the overhanging foliage will provide extra protection. The bright yellow flower spikes of some of these hybrids draw the attention into the deep shadows.

IN PARTIAL SHADE

Most gardens have areas with partial shade. This may come from a light canopy of tree ferns or palms or may be an area with full morning sun followed by complete shade from a house or fence later in the day. Or perhaps the edges of a group of trees where the sun will only reach when it is low in the morning or afternoon.

Fortunately, the largest group of bromeliads are those that prefer some shade. Many of these will still grow well in full shade, but achieve their best colour with some direct or filtered sun. Nearly all of them will burn in full sun, although a few will acclimatise over time, but with a quite different foliage form and colour.

Many of the larger aechmeas do well in partial shade: *Aechmea caudata* and its beautiful variegated form are at their best in bright filtered light. Too much shade and

Top: An array of bromeliads with exotics such as the Australian Grass Tree form an excellent border to this formal path. Above: A bed of *Aechmea cylindrata* hybrid flowering en masse is quite impressive.

Above: *Aechmea* 'Exotica Mystique' can reach up to 1.5 m wide and over 1 m tall, even when not in flower.

these plants look leggy and messy; too much sun and they become stressed and yellow. This species is tough enough to be used on cliff faces with ease, and will choke other plants out so plant it where you need good weed control.

For a touch of drama, use the big aechmeas such as *A. fendleri*, *A. lueddemanniana* 'Rubra' and *A. mexicana*. All of these have the most majestic flower spikes with dramatically coloured berries which remain in colour for months. They look fantastic under the dappled shade of big palms, but be aware that each plant can reach 1 m diameter so give them plenty of room to expand. All three develop their best leaf colour when exposed to the maximum amount of light possible, without direct sun; *A. lueddemanniana* becoming very dark and *A. mexicana*

Below: The shocking pink of *Aechmea fasciata* can be seen from many metres away, making it ideal for highlighting slightly shady gardens.

taking on a bronze hue. Once established, they will reward you with regular flowering every summer.

Another big aechmea that likes partial shade is *A. pectinata*, which can reach a span of 1.5 m if grown in the right situation. Try these large plants at the bottom of a garden or patio staircase, where you can see them as you go down the steps — the shocking-pink splashes of colour look magnificent when viewed from above.

Equally as large and impressive as *A. pectinata*, *A.* 'Burgundy' prefers a position further into the shrubbery. It develops its glossy, dark burgundy leaves best in shade, but still needs some light to stop it getting leggy. It looks stunning rising out of a bed of deep green mondo grass.

The smaller aechmeas also have their place in the partially shady areas of the garden. *A. apocalyptica*, *A. calyculata* and *A. winkleri* will all provide very effective groundcover under trees and brighten up the garden over winter with their fiery flowers of red, orange, blue and

yellow. They are best in dappled light, although they can quite easily adapt to several hours of direct sun in the morning or late afternoon.

A. 'Covata' and A. fasciata make an interesting combination in the partial shade. Both are epiphytic and so can be planted where there is very little soil, over rocks or retaining walls; they also form quite dense clumps which will sprawl over anything in their way, making for lovely curvaceous edges. Both these species will grow in full shade and full sun but their appearance changes dramatically in the different conditions, and they tend to look their best in dappled light. In heavy shade they have very open and quite lush-looking rosettes, whereas in full sun the rosettes become much more compact, spiky looking with very little green left. The flowers are the most exciting feature of these species: the bright pink pyramids of A. fasciata can be seen from a considerable distance, and once the clump is established they are quite free flowering and long lasting so there is colour virtually all year round.

Above: A cluster of *Cryptanthus* form a groundcover with *Peperomia*.

For low-growing groundcover, it is difficult to go past *Cryptanthus*, or the 'Earth Stars' as they are commonly called. These little gems propagate so freely that they can quickly cover an empty space with their unusual foliage. Fantastic in small spaces, such as edges of paths, they will conform to the shape over time. They are best planted in the foreground as they tend to be lost among bigger plants. *Cryptanthus* 'Cascade' is also well suited to planting around edges, as the pups on long stolons will clamber through and over any rocks or similar forms.

The bromeliads probably most suited to growing in partial shade are the neoregelias — they simply thrive in dappled light. In very light shade, or where there is only shade for the midday period in summer, the heavily coloured species like the following are simply standouts.

Neoregelia 'Crimson Nest' lives up to its name, one of the best for vivid crimson colour in the garden. It will still colour up in heavier shade, but with less intensity. *N.* 'Sailors Warning' can take almost full sun. A deep orange-red hybrid, such as *N.* 'Apricot Beauty', looks superb underplanted with bright green *Scleranthus*; it is very sensitive to light levels and will only achieve the full glow in very high light; however, full sun may burn it. *N.* 'Stoplight' is similar, looking its best with only a small amount of shade.

Some species of *Nidularium* such as *N. terminale* and *N. procerum* are mostly native to coastal Brazil where they can be found as a groundcover and over low objects such as fallen trees, rocks and shrubs. This is also ideal in the garden and drifts of these plants can look very attractive, placed near and over stumps for example. Although they are shade lovers, these plants can take some direct sun in the morning and late afternoon; in fact their foliage takes on much more colour when grown in these conditions.

Dappled light is ideal for the patterned-leaved vrieseas, many of which show their best colour when grown in partial shade. The most sumptuous combination in the garden would have to be large lush palms or cycads underplanted with *Vriesea hieroglyphica*, *V. platynema*, *V. platynema* var. *variegata*, or one of the many *V. fosteriana* hybrids.

Another large plant suitable for partial shade is the beautiful *Wittrockia* 'Leopardinum', which can take a range of light levels, looking fantastic in all. The mottling on this hybrid is superb, as good as any vriesea.

IN SUNNY GARDENS

Sunny areas are a feature of many gardens, whether it be an open landscape surrounding a pool or lawn, or a totally sunny garden by a beach or lake. But many of the plants we use for these gardens wilt and burn in the scorching heat and blazing sun, not to mention the dry hard clay or sandy soils.

Many people find the solution to this is to plant desert, Californian or Mediterranean-style gardens, and these are becoming quite popular for their dramatic appearance and low maintenance. Bromeliads are an often overlooked group

This page, top: Two splashes of deep red *Neoregelia* lift this contemporary garden.
Above: The glossy, mottled leaves of *Wittrockia* 'Leopardinum' shine from a leafy hollow.

Opposite, top: *Nidularium terminale* is quite well suited to bright shade.
Bottom: Mixed bromeliads with succulents in light shade.

of plants also suitable for sunny sites. There is a huge number of bromeliads that thrive in desert or beach-type conditions; indeed, many well-known bromeliads are native to such famous beaches as Copacabana and the Baja Peninsula.

Many of the bromeliads suited to these arid conditions are also very cold hardy, so are not just restricted to subtropical and tropical regions. This is not surprising, as in their native desert or grassland environment, overnight temperatures can drop well below freezing. Some, such as *Bromelia balansae* and *Puya mirabilis* can cope with -10°C without damage. These are perfect for seasonally dry cold areas such as the Canterbury plains and volcanic plateau of New Zealand, or central and southern Texas and the southern cities of New Mexico and Arizona in the United States.

The whole *Puya* genus is exceptionally well suited to the desert or beach-style garden. Most come from the Andean highlands at altitudes of 3–5000 m above sea level, and are so tough they can be grown just about anywhere. Most are very large plants and very well protected with spines; however, there are a few smaller species, such as *Puya*

mirabilis, which has numerous thin silver-green leaves up to 50 cm long. Puyas have some of the most unusual flowers in the Bromeliad family and *P. mirabilis* is no exception, with scented greenish white flowers. However, the most unusual would have to be *P. alpestris*, with its unearthly torquoise flowers.

Some beach gardens extend right down into the sand dunes and are frequently planted with exotic plants to give more of a holiday feel to a beach house. Plants used this way need to be tough enough to survive neglect, drought, salt spray and the occasional bashing with four-wheel drives. Many bromeliad species will survive quite well in this situation, but for real toughness, both the puyas and bromelias will fit the bill.

Bromelia species, such as *B. balansae* and others are among the toughest of all plants. Use these like you would *Agave americana*: that is, plant them where they have room to move, as they clump vigorously. Preferably, plant them on a mound out of the way of children or passers-by, as the large rosettes up to 1.5 m diameter are edged in vicious curved spines and tipped with near daggers. In South America, rows of these are used around isolated properties to keep out both two-legged and four-legged predators — this is worth taking note of, as the plants are much more effective and attractive than coils of razor wire!

Dyckia species are often grown with succulents and cacti, as their stiff spiky leaves fit in well. Most species are reasonably small, although there are a few bigger, more imposing species for the larger garden. Over time, the plants will form tight mounds of spiky leaves and in summer the flower spikes are provided generously, mostly in yellows and oranges. These plants are very tough, many of them native to southern South America, making them suitable for temperate gardens.

This page, top right: Tough red neoregelias such as these are indispensable in sunny gardens.
Right: Red *Neoregelia* and *Aechmea distichantha* work well together in this sunny landscape.

Opposite, top: *Puya venusta* is a moderate-sized puya which is noted for its vibrant red and blue flowerhead.
Bottom: A fierce landscape of *Puya* and *Aloe bainesii*.

This page, top: *Alcantarea imperialis* 'Rubra' has sufficient impact to carry off any situation.
Above: *Vriesea fosteriana* 'Rubra' look almost prehistoric with these moa in a beachside garden.

Opposite, top: *Neoregelia* hybrids form a vibrant groundcover next to a rocky pool.
Bottom: This *Neoregelia cruenta* hybrid is very sun tolerant and suitable for planting in the open next to ponds.

Some of the toughest aechmeas are *Aechmea distichantha* and its hybrids, which form large, spiky silver-grey plants up to 1.5 m high, with needle-sharp terminal spines. The stunning flower spikes can be seen from some distance and last for months. Try planting them surrounded by *A. recurvata* as a groundcover.

A. recurvata and its varieties are also exceptionally hardy. They are much smaller plants and are great for planting on driftwood for a beach look, or using as drifts of colour over shells or pebbles. During flowering, which usually occurs in summer, the rosettes of spiny grey-green foliage change colour, and the plants can even look as if they are sprayed with lacquer. Depending on the variety, the plants will turn bright pink, fire-engine red, purple or even charcoal when flowering.

A. callichroma is another imposing plant for a hot sunny garden. They look great as a massed clump of slightly bronzed olive-green leaves among rocks or at the back of a mixed border. The long-lasting flowers come up in great drifts of yellow. Mix them with the glossy orange foliage and vibrant red and yellow flowers of *A. blanchetiana* for some wonderful blending of leaf colour.

Alcantarea imperialis 'Rubra' would have to be the plant of the moment. Although it looks tropical, it is in fact very tough, handling full sun, salt spray and drought with ease. This bromeliad can reach a span of more than 1.5 m, although it takes up to 10 years to get to this size. The thick red flower spike reaches up to 2.5 m in height, producing hundreds of slightly fragrant white flowers. In full sun, the leaves take on a deep red cast. Try these as a matching pair flanking a door, gateway or on opposite corners of a swimming pool. There cannot be a more imposing and dramatic entranceway than two of these in or out of flower.

Despite their reputation as shade lovers, there are several *Vriesea* species and hybrids which look absolutely exquisite in full sun, the most notable being *V. fosteriana* 'Rubra'. In the shade, this plant has lovely markings of reddish brown interspersed with green. However, in the sun the reddish brown turns a rich chocolate and the green becomes almost nonexistent, with just a hint of cream banding to break the brown. For a striking contrast,

This page, top: *Neoregelia* 'Sugar and Spice' is a tough little plant that can handle just about anything.
Above: For intense colour in full sun, the very tough *Neoregelia olens* 'Vulcan' is ideal.

Opposite: Red-leaved *Neoregelia* hybrids are ideal for this situation.

team it up with the white form *V. fosteriana* 'Vista'.

The neoregelias mustn't be overlooked for this style of garden either; with their flat rosettes and brightly coloured foliage, they add the sizzle to any hot garden. Not all species are suited to full sun though, so be careful when selecting plants — in general the neoregelias with heavily patterned, leathery foliage are best suited, while the types with softer, shinier leaves are best kept under light shade and away from frost.

Some tried and true *Neoregelia* species include *N.* 'Julian Nally' with its marbled maroon and green leaves, and *N.* 'Mottles' with its stout, heavily mottled leaves of dark maroon. The harsher the environment, the brighter the maroon speckling, and the same goes with all the *N. marmorata* hybrids. *N. chlorosticta* and its hybrids are also ideal; these are small plants, but the colourful rosettes of peppered red leaves add colour and interest.

Any hardy garden should have a drift of *N. concentrica* hybrids with their large, tough rosettes of leathery leaves which are usually heavily blotched with dark purple to black markings. These markings intensify in harsh conditions. At flowering the centre turns rich purple, shocking pink, deep blue or glorious red depending on the variety. They may need a little shade over the midday, as the wide leaves can scorch in summer. Fabulous around pools, as are most bromeliads, they stay neat and tidy for much longer than other plant species and provide year-round interest.

N. 'Noble Descent' is an excellent hybrid which provides a good contrast to most other neoregelias. Light green leaves, which turn almost yellow in strong light, provide a background for light speckles of red, with red leaf tips and a red centre at flowering. The red form of *N. cruenta* is also a stunning plant. The upper surface of the leathery leaves is a dark speckled red, while the underside is barred with silver.

Some of the miniature neoregelias are also great for hot gardens. Hybrids with 'Fireball' as a parent are particularly good, showing their best colours when in full sun and harsh conditions. These plants can also be finishing details by being planted as epiphytes on stumps, driftwood or even on mooring posts! For a cooler touch,

try mixing a few N. *chlorosticta* 'Marble Throat', with their snow-coloured centres.

When selecting neoregelias for hot sunny spots, gardeners in New Zealand and parts of Australia need to take the intensity of the UV radiation into account. Plants grown in high UV areas are much more likely to suffer from sunburn than in their native habitat.

The design of your desert-style garden needs to be well thought out as these hardy bromeliads are not plants easily shifted. Points to consider include drainage, soil type, weed control, contour of the garden and eventual plant size (remember some bromeliads clump vigorously). Keep in mind particular foibles of some plants, for example, *Bromelia balansae* sends out very strong suckers some distance, so unless you want these growing up to your front door, make sure there is some barrier, for example boulders, a drain, retaining wall or the like.

It is a good idea to wear leather gloves and canvas arm protectors when dealing with the bigger more vicious types. Make sure you get in early with weed control; spraying or digging out perennial weeds is a must before planting as weed control becomes very difficult later. Covering the soil with a layer of stones or pebbles is always a good idea with bromeliads, as the stones help retain heat overnight and moisture during dry periods. A layer of stones will also help suppress the weeds, particularly if several layers of newspaper are laid underneath. Once the planting is finished, set up your hammock with a good view of the garden and enjoy, as your garden work is done for the next few years.

AS EPIPHYTES

In all kinds of gardens, but particularly when planted as epiphytes, bromeliads can add the finishing touch. As much as a house isn't a home until the paintings and ornaments are placed attractively, so a garden isn't finished until the bromeliads and other small exotics are planted.

One of the more appealing features of bromeliads is their ability to be grown in trees or stumps, adding an extra dimension to the garden. Instead of just growing small plants at ground level with larger shrubs and trees as a backdrop, you can also have the trunks and branches festooned with colourful bromeliads. This is a wonderful way of adding colour and interest and bringing a sense of mystery to any garden. The foliage looks great all year round and the seasonal flowering can produce striking highlights.

Many evergreen trees such as macadamia, avocado, citrus, *Metrosideros*, *Ficus* and *Banksia* have a tendency to produce a number of low-angled branches from the same point, forming nice nest areas in the fork to place clumps of the larger-growing bromeliads, and just about any plant will look great in these. Focus on the patterned-leaved vrieseas such as *Vriesea fenestralis*, *V. glutinosa*, *V. fosteriana* 'Red Chestnut', *V. hieroglyphica* or *V. fosteriana* for dramatic leaves. The leaf markings on these plants all look stunning when seen from the side or from below, even more so than when viewed from above.

Large *Neoregelia* species are impressive also when placed in trees. A species such as *N. pascoaliana* really only shows its best colours when seen from below, while the under-leaf silver banding of *N. spectabilis* is often overlooked if planted at ground level.

In their native habitats such as South America, many bromeliad hosts are deciduous; however, beware that in temperate climates such as New Zealand, many of the deciduous trees used as hosts drop too many large leaves at once, which can clog up the plants causing them to rot.

Deciduous trees such as cherries, willow and jacaranda take billbergias best, as they cope well with the change in light levels between seasons and the slender rosettes tend to clog less than more open types. Also, the beautiful

This page, above: A well-established clump of huge *Neoregelia* 'Rosy Morn' sits atop a tree fern stump.

Opposite, top left: A tangle of driftwood has *Tillandsia* species casually draped over it, with a large flowering *Vriesea hieroglyphica* planted alongside. Top right: Even large species such as *Aechmea pectinata* grow well as epiphytes. Bottom right: *Billbergia* flowers often hang down lower than the plant, making them wonderful for planting in trees.

hanging flowers of *Billbergia* usually appear in late winter or early spring, before the leaves have returned. Many different types of *Billbergia* can be planted in larger trees, and as each species has a slightly different flowering period, two to three months of glorious flowering in shades of pink, red, orange and scarlet can be expected. The flowers often hang down lower than the plant, a bonus when planting in trees.

Like the *Billbergia*, many of the *Vriesea* genus have hanging flowers. These are ideal for placing high in the trees, or at the top of banks or tree stumps. The vibrant flowers of *V. simplex* and the soft pink of *V. guttata* are at their best when viewed from the side or from underneath. The deep purple hanging spike of *V.* 'Sanderiana' is quite sumptuous displayed like this also.

One of the best bromeliads for flowering displays is *Aechmea nudicaulis* and its hybrids, which flower just on Christmas in the southern hemisphere, with numerous spikes of scarlet and yellow, just right for the season. These tough tubular plants look fantastic when allowed to

Top: A 20-year-old clump of *Aechmea nudicaulis* in full flower right on Christmas Day. Above: A mix of sun-hardy *Neoregelia* and *Tillandsia* thrive on this fallen log.

clump up on a tree. *A. racinae* is commonly known as Christmas Jewels in the northern hemisphere, as it flowers almost exactly on Christmas Day. This is a much softer plant than *A. nudicaulis*, but equally suited to planting as an epiphyte, as long as it stays in the shade. It has very similar colouration and a pendulous flower spike. With both of them in the garden, both the winter solstice and Christmas can be celebrated, no matter which hemisphere you are in!

Instead of hiring expensive machinery to take out large tree stumps and boulders, make a talking point of them by covering them with bromeliads. However, be aware that as most stumps and boulders are out in the open, hardy bromeliads are needed. This is where the spiky aechmeas come into their own. Species such as *Aechmea recurvata*, *A. pineliana*, and *A.* 'Covata' are all tough enough, and *A. orlandiana* shows off its colour best when grown hard and in full sun, perfect for this situation. Also, the hardy *Neoregelia* species, such as *N. marmorata*, *N. princeps* and *N.* 'Aztec' provide their best leaf colour when grown in full sun.

All types of tree ferns, living or dead, make ideal hosts for epiphytic bromeliads. The woolly, fibrous trunk tree ferns like *Dicksonia fibrosa* are great for small *Tillandsia*, *Vriesea* and *Guzmania* species, which can be planted directly into the fibre. Clumping tree ferns such as *Dicksonia squarrosa* form natural nesting areas between the stems which larger bromeliads can be placed on. Hard trunk species, such as the common black tree fern, can be used to grow bromeliads that spread via stolons like *Neoregelia ampullacea* and its hybrids — these will quickly spread around and up the trunk.

The holes left in the top of tree fern stumps once they have died are tailor-made for larger bromeliads like the big vrieseas, such as *Vriesea hieroglyphica*, *V. fosteriana* 'Rubra' and *V. platynema*. These species are mostly quite hardy, withstanding several degrees of frost and quite a bit of sun, and the large rosettes and heavily patterned foliage look stunning on the stump of a tree fern. On really big stumps, the giant bromeliads like *Alcantarea imperialis* 'Rubra' are in a league of their own.

Some palms are also excellent for planting epiphytic

bromeliads. Large *Phoenix reclinata*, *P. canariensis* and *Butia capitata* form handy pockets that can be used to grow many types of bromeliads. *Trachycarpus fortunei* has a fibrous trunk, similar to *Dicksonia fibrosa*, which can be used for small bromeliads such as *Tillandsia*. As this palm provides less shade than a *Dicksonia*, small highly coloured neoregelias could be used, like *Neoregelia* 'Fireball' and its hybrids. One of the best hybrids for growing as an

Above left: This *Neoregelia* hybrid has long stolons, which make it very useful as a climbing epiphyte.
Above: Clusters of red-leaved *Neoregelia* and silver *Tillandsia* look great on these tree fern trunks.

epiphyte is the gorgeous little N. 'Short & Sweet'. This tiny jewel displays its best colours when grown in a tough situation, so plant in full sun on trees, tree fern stumps or in hanging baskets.

Cacti are an interesting and seldom-used group of plants for growing epiphytic bromeliads on. In their natural environment, quite a few of the *Tillandsia* are found growing on the larger cacti. If you have a large, well-established columnar type cactus, such as *Trichocereus pachanoi*, look for wounds or breaks that have healed over — the tillandsias can be glued straight into these spots and will happily grow without affecting the cactus.

Rock or concrete walls can also be used to grow *Tillandsia* and *Vriesea* species. This is a wonderful way of covering an unsightly area and turning it into a feature instead, and is simply a matter of glueing the plants directly onto the rocks or concrete. It is even easier when the surface is rough or chipped. Remember to water these

Above: A *Vriesea* hybrid, *Neoregelia* hybrid and staghorn ferns race to climb this *Trachycarpus* trunk.
Right: *Billbergia nutans* and B. 'Hoelscheriana' swathe this *Butia* palm in pink and scarlet.

often though, as a sheer wall may not receive much rainfall.

Another rather unique way of drawing the eye away from an unsightly area is to place a living curtain of xerophytic tillandsias in front of it. Instead of mounting the plants on trees or stumps, either hang them directly from strands of thin nylon fishing line, or attach them to a small piece of driftwood or similar and hang that. With clusters of *Tillandsia* at varying heights and thick strands of *T. usneoides* providing the density, a living curtain can soon be created, which will gently sway in the breeze.

Another appealing feature of many of the xerophytic tillandsias is their ability to form a clump in the shape of a ball. To achieve this effect, attach the plant to a piece of

Above: Over time, these recently planted strings of *Tillandsia* species will form a lovely curtain.
Top right: *Tillandsia stricta* gradually develops dense balls of stiff silver leaves.
Right: An aerial garden of ferns, *Tillandsia*, *Neoregelia* and *Aechmea* species.

nylon and let it grow for six months or so. Then take it down and attach the nylon to another section, so the clump hangs at a different angle forcing the new growth in the new direction. Over time, and with patience, a perfect ball of foliage can be created and looks fantastic when in flower. Small species such as *T. tenuifolia*, *T. recurvata* and *T. stricta* are especially good for this.

When planting an epiphyte tree, try to achieve balance in the planting. Use an odd number of plants, ie one, three, five or more; and take their eventual size into account. Larger plants will usually look better at the bottom of the tree with smaller ones nearer the top.

Attaching and looking after epiphytic bromeliads is as easy as falling off a log! It is best to plant in spring or autumn, when conditions are most favourable for root growth and the weather is not either too cold or too sunny for the plants to cope with.

Above: Although on the ground now, these stoloniferous *Neoregelia pineliana* will climb any object nearby.
Left: These *Tillandsia somnians* have been attached using staples and wire over the long stolons.

Clumping plants, such as *Neoregelia pascoaliana* should be placed near their final position, as these won't move much. Stoloniferous plants (those which spread via short woody stems), like many of the *Billbergia*, some *Nidularium*, some *Neoregelia* and some *Vriesea* species, should be planted lower in the tree. They can then climb the trunk or branch as they grow.

When attaching plants on fibrous trunks such as tree ferns, just make a hole and place the base of the bromeliad in the hole. If necessary it can be secured with plastic-coated wire wrapped around the trunk at the level of the hole. Or, liberally smear half the inside of the hole with a glue like Liquid Nails™ or silicone sealer. Don't do the whole area, as the hole will become watertight and may rot the plant.

In palm pockets, just wedge the bromeliad in the pocket with its base or root system in contact with the leaf mould already in there.

When placing bromeliads on hard trunks or in tree forks, first wrap the root system in sphagnum moss or coconut fibre and bind it with plastic-coated wire. Then use this wire to attach the clump to the fork or trunk. An alternative method is to hammer in large staples, which works well when attaching a stoloniferous type — the staple can go over the stolon. Alternatively, wrap pantyhose around the base.

For varieties that form little or no roots, like some tillandsias, a glue such as Liquid Nails™ can be used to attach the plant to the trunk or other object. Cover any visible glue with shredded sphagnum moss.

Once the epiphyte is in place, water at least weekly, with a spray over the foliage and the base of the plant. This will help the new root system become established and attach to the tree. It typically takes about six months for the plants to become securely attached to the host plant.

One technique that increases the chances of attachment, is to ensure that the heel of the plant (actually shaped like an elbow) which is found near the base of the offshoots is hard up against the trunk. Pups are generally more successful as they are vigorous in producing new root systems; often the mother plants are incapable of producing new roots, with all their energies going into

flower, seed or pup production. Where a mother plant is used, try to tie it on with any pups present close to the trunk, as it will be these that attach rather than the mother plant.

Remember, if wire is used to secure bromeliads, remove it once the plants have attached themselves, or at least after a year, otherwise the host plant will be strangled.

Something to remember is, over time, some bromeliad clumps become very heavy. I distinctly recall an incident when visiting my mother at our family home, where I hadn't been for some months. Just after I arrived, on a completely windless night with a light drizzle falling, I heard a loud crack and a whoosh sound, as if someone had thrown a large bucket of water out. The next morning all was revealed — a clump of *Aechmea nudicaulis* that I had planted in a lemon tree some 20 years earlier had decided to choose that moment to split the tree and crash down. The whoosh was many litres of water emptying out from the plants.

The weight becomes more of a problem when the host plant is weakened, or is already dead, in the case of tree fern stumps and driftwood. Where they enter the ground is a prime spot for rot, so keep an eye out — a technique for avoiding this is to cement the base of the stump or driftwood where it enters the ground. If the cement comes above the ground a couple of centimetres, this will delay the rotting process.

ON ROCKS

In their natural habitat bromeliads are often found growing on rocks, and in fact some species grow only on rocks. In the mountain ranges of Mexico, the Andes and the Tepui of Venezuela and Guyana, whole mountains are dominated by species of bromeliads. Even on flat granite slabs that are barren of other life, clumps of hardy *Aechmea* can be found. By the coast, more bromeliads can be found clinging to life on cliff faces, sometimes splashed by storm surf and lashed by high winds.

This habit of some bromeliads of growing on rocks can be used to great effect in the garden. First, suitable rocks must be found. Although some bromeliads will grow on smooth granite, soft, textured or porous rocks offer a

much better chance of success for the home gardener. Volcanic rocks such as scoria are ideal, as the roots can easily take hold, and soft rocks like shale and sandstone are also excellent as they can be carved to accommodate the plants.

An important thing to bear in mind is the stability of the rock. If it doesn't have a flat base, it will need to be dug into the ground to prevent it toppling when the plants grow.

The plants themselves can be attached with a glue such as Liquid Nails™. Some people advise drilling a hole in the rock first to put the base of the plant in, but this may hold water which can rot the base, so it is usually better to glue the plant onto the rock without drilling first. Any visible glue can be covered with shredded sphagnum moss or dust from the rock itself. Over time, plant roots and stolons will anchor the clump to the rock and also hide any glue.

There are many bromeliads that will look great on rocks, but it is important to match the size of the rocks with the plants, otherwise the planting can look contrived. Take into account the colour of the rock as well, when choosing plants. A red scoria rock will look best with silver- or green-leaved plants, while a pale sandstone will look stunning with red-leaved plants. Textured rocks such as rain-carved limestone boulders are fantastic with bromeliads.

A mixed clump of small *Vriesea* such as *V. corcovadensis*, *V. vagans* or *V. flammea* look good on a small football-size rock, where they can clump over the top, and they show their best leaf colour in adverse conditions, so the rock environment is ideal. Larger plants such as *Aechmea nudicaulis* or *A. distichantha* will need progressively larger rocks to grow over. Equally impressive is a hard rock such as granite, with nothing but a tenacious bromeliad clinging to the side or the top, giving the impression of life on the edge of survival.

On some types of rocks, mosses and lichens will thrive next to bromeliads, and they add a feeling of permanence to the arrangement. To achieve this look faster, a shortcut is to throw some moss, lichen and yoghurt, diluted with water into a blender, then spray or paint the blend onto the

This page, above: A deep wine-coloured *Neoregelia* hybrid fills the crack between two rocks and sets off the surrounding plants nicely.

Opposite, top: *Neoregelia* 'Mottles' and *Aechmea* 'Covata' clamber over a small peak of volcanic rocks.
Bottom: This brightly coloured *Neoregelia ampullacea* hybrid is simply stunning on top of the rock.

rock. Lightly mist with water each day for a couple of weeks and you will find the growth is much quicker.

One of the benefits of growing bromeliads on rocks is that they can be shifted around and displayed in much the same way as pots, certainly this is the case for smaller rocks. If you plan to move them around, consider using a board attached with resin or glue as the base.

Many bromeliads in the wild are found scrambling through fissures and crevices in rocky cliff faces and rock falls. Create this look in a larger rock feature with many rocks interspersed with crevices and small plateaus of soil — planting bromeliads among them can create one of the most stunning effects in the garden, as they smooth off the rough edges of the formation and give it a permanent appearance. Virtually any bromeliad species can be planted in rock features like this, simply match the size and type of plant to the amount of soil available to it. However, the best effect will be achieved with bromeliads that spread via stolons or suckers, as they will scramble through and over the rocks searching out new pockets of

nutrients. *Orthophytum saxicola* is a very good example of this, as the little spiky orange rosettes will quickly spread through the crevices, filling any available crack and fissure, and look fantastic over pale rocks like sandstone. A true cliff dweller such as *Fascicularia bicolor* always looks at home on a steep rock bank, and their roots will find their way between the rocks as the plants spread via their sprawling stems.

Another interesting, but completely different look can be achieved by using the tall tubes of *Quesnelia marmorata*. This dark mottled plant spreads by thick stolons, making a network of linked tubes. The stolons are quite fascinating the way they creep over the rocks, bending to every curve and angle.

On a shaded bank of rocks, soft-leaved bromeliads such as *Canistropsis billbergioides* will clamber up using their long stolons, to eventually cover the entire bank. This is a great way of softening a retaining wall and even better if a soft creeping fern like the maidenhair fern (*Asplenium hispidulum*) or the rabbit's foot fern (*Davallia* spp) is included in the design.

IN TROPICAL GARDENS & HOTHOUSES

For gardeners in temperate climates, a tropical garden is often highly desirable, and many bromeliads will do just as well, or even better outdoors in a temperate or subtropical climate as they would in a greenhouse. In fact, although many people consider bromeliads as tropical plants, many actually produce their best colour out of the tropics. This is clearly seen in countries that span the tropic to temperate latitudes, like Australia. In the far north of Australia, a number of neoregelia hybrids fail to produce the leaf colours that they can achieve in more temperate southern states such as New South Wales. The reason for this is mostly to do with night temperatures. In the tropics, overnight temperatures do not fall sufficiently low to allow maximum development of anthocyanin, which is what produces the brilliant reds seen in neoregelias grown in cooler climates.

However, if you are gardening in a temperate climate, there are still a significant number of bromeliads that are

Below: An overwhelmingly lush, shady subtropical landscape.

Above: This lush growth is best achieved in a greenhouse or tropical garden. Right: *Vriesea zamorensis* is an ideal subject for a tropical garden or greenhouse.

best grown as indoor pot plants or in the greenhouse. Many of these originate from the large European breeders and are bred for indoor use, such as *Guzmania* 'Ultra', G. 'Mandarine' and G. 'Pax'. Others are species from the tropical jungles that are simply unable to adapt to cooler climates, like *Vriesea zamorensis* and *Aechmea chantinii*. If these plants are grown outside, even where there is no frost, they are likely to show cold damage over winter if temperatures fall below 5°C for more than a few hours. In a greenhouse though, these plants will thrive and it is possible for gardeners even in the coldest climates to create their own piece of tropical jungle. Often the tropical

Above: *Guzmania zahnii* 'Variegata' is really only suitable for tropical gardens or heated greenhouses.

bromeliads are some of the showiest, as in their native habitat they have to compete for pollination with many other very brightly coloured plants and frequently with considerable shade.

Many tropical bromeliads available now have been extensively hybridised, so an enthusiast can create a showpiece that is much more colourful and vibrant than any natural jungle could be. In the darkest depths of the tropical garden clusters of brilliantly coloured *Guzmania* can be planted on trees, perched on tree fern stumps or planted in the ground itself. The colours of the modern hybrids are so bright that the dark areas will seem to be the lightest. The same applies to any *Vriesea* 'Poelmanii' hybrids. These spears of glossy red look like flames when planted among thick foliage.

Aechmea chantinii comes from tropical jungles and prefers this environment. It is spectacular with the silver banding underneath the leaves and its glorious inflorescence, and it looks great as an epiphyte over fallen logs or stumps, or as an indoor potted plant.

Another unique way of growing bromeliads is in terrariums. Terrariums have evolved from simple habitats for plants, or lizards, frogs and various other wildlife in glass tanks, to complex ecosystems, often incorporating tropical fish pools and habitats for amphibious or terrestrial creatures, and bromeliads are tailor-made for this. They are becoming increasingly popular in large cities where people want a small slice of the jungle to take them temporarily away from the hustle and bustle of the city.

Terrariums are ideal for growing the smaller, more tender bromeliads such as *Cryptanthus* and small *Guzmania* or *Vriesea* species, which thrive on the humidity and temperature generated in this environment. As most of the fish and other animals that are grown in these tanks are tropical or subtropical in origin, the tanks are usually kept at a temperature and humidity level ideal for many bromeliads. Most terrariums use glass fish tanks, and often when amphibious animals are kept, or some area of terrestrial rather than aquatic plant life is needed, a raised platform will be installed. This could be of a large rock or piece of driftwood sticking out of the water, onto which bromeliads can be glued. Or it may be a piece of horizontal glass glued to the side of the tank, which can then be covered in potting mix, driftwood and plants. Another idea would be to glue pieces of cork bark, coconut husk or tree fern to the sides — the plants can then be attached to these.

IN POTS

Most bromeliads make fantastic pot plants, either indoors or out; in fact some of the best bromeliads I have seen were grown as indoor plants in a window facing the morning sun. For those gardens with limited space, potted bromeliads are ideal, as they can be grown in hanging baskets or narrow planter boxes.

One of the main advantages to growing bromeliads in pots is that they can be shifted around. In warm temperate or subtropical gardens, this can be used to great effect by changing the look of the garden at whim, so is great for those restless gardeners who always dig up and shift plants. As the plants come into flower or full colour they can be moved into more prominent positions, and those plants that need some work on them, or which are not in full colour, can be placed further back until later.

For gardeners in cool temperate climates or in locations with very cold winters, potted bromeliads are ideal. Over summer the plants can live outdoors, taking advantage of the rain to grow to their best and livening up the garden with their glorious colours and tropical foliage.

Apartment balconies are also often ideal for bromeliads. With a large potted palm or similar to provide some dappled light, a collection of bromeliads can be brought out each spring to enjoy the milder weather and encourage people outside into the instant tropical garden. During the colder months, the plants can be brought inside, where they will provide a much needed lift for the monotony of winter. Many bromeliads are winter flowering, so there will always be some colour to brighten the room, and the lower light levels in winter offers a slightly drier situation, beneficial until the spring growth starts.

Many bromeliads are quite happy to live all year round indoors and they are some of the most suited plants to indoor growing, which is why so many millions of them are grown each year in Europe and the United States. The most common genera for year-round indoors are *Guzmania*, *Vriesea* and *Nidularium*, which all adapt readily to low-light situations.

Right: A large potted *Vriesea fosteriana* 'Rubra' contrasts well with the soft green foliage in the background.
Below: New *Neoregelia* hybrids such as 'Scarlet Charlotte' are used extensively in interior planting.

However, the range of bromeliads that can be grown indoors is not only limited to these commercially produced species and hybrids. Over time, a collection of such diverse genera as *Aechmea*, *Tillandsia*, *Dyckia*, *Neoregelia* and even *Puya* can be grown indoors, although the latter usually only in very sunny and spacious situations.

All of these bromeliads need to be given the same consideration for such things as light and temperature as outdoor-grown plants. Plants that are best grown in full sun will not look their best in a dark bathroom, and plants that need tropical conditions will not do well on an exposed Chicago balcony in early spring.

As well as this, some thought must also be given to the special needs of bromeliads indoors. Firstly, it should be remembered that leaf scorching may be worse through a window in mid-summer than in the open garden, as plants are less able to cool themselves indoors — net curtains, vertical or venetian blinds can often effectively avoid this problem.

Light levels can change quite dramatically from season to season through windows, with the changing angle of the sun. Keep an eye on your plants as the season progresses and be prepared to shift them if necessary. Indirect light is very common indoors and can be quite bright. A number of the shade-loving, or partial shade-loving bromeliads will do quite well, as bright indirect light is sufficient.

Air movement assumes more importance for bromeliads grown indoors, particularly for the more xerophytic species of *Tillandsia* and *Vriesea*. Without good air movement, these plants will become much more susceptible to disease and insect attack. Fresh air also provides some of their nitrogen requirement and all of their carbon dioxide requirement. Always try to have some open windows, or a fan nearby if the outside air is too cold. Alternatively, place the plants near doorways, where good air movement is more likely.

Top left: Large *Neoregelia* like these make excellent potted specimens.
Left: In addition to support and mulching, these white stones provide the finishing touch to this arrangement with *Vriesea fosteriana* 'Rubra'.

Watering indoor plants poses some special problems. Many houses are now climate controlled using air conditioning, which is often set at a relative humidity level of 60% or less, too low for many bromeliads. Daily misting with rainwater is well advised in these situations.

As indoor growing is most common in large cities, where the quality of tap water is typically not suitable for bromeliads, you would be well advised to use room-temperature rainwater or from a water purifier.

One of the most important things to remember when planting bromeliads in pots is to select the right size pot for the plant. Contrary to popular belief, it is not always ideal to have a large bromeliad in a small pot. In fact, although the comment is often made that a particular bromeliad looks 'overpotted', this is almost never the case, except where the pot is so large that the plants cannot utilise all the space and the mix becomes sour.

Some genera, typically the terrestrial types like *Dyckia*, *Puya*, *Hechtia* and *Pitcairnia*, have quite a large root system and quickly become potbound and stressed if they are in a small pot. Often the brown tips these plants get is due to the small size of the pot, which prevents the potting mix letting sufficient water through the dense foliage.

Even epiphytic types such as *Vriesea* and green-leafed *Tillandsia* will do better in a larger pot than a smaller one. Of course, another reason for choosing a larger pot is stability — there is nothing worse than having to continually rescue bromeliads that have fallen over in high winds because their pot was pathetically small.

However, there are some instances when a small pot produces a better result. For example, many of the *Billbergia* achieve their best colour when the root system is somewhat constricted.

Bromeliads can be grown in virtually any type of pot. Plastic pots are useful for their low cost and light weight, great if you use potted bromeliads for instant colour in your garden. These can be shifted and replaced as each plant comes into colour, making your garden a showpiece all year round. When placing in the garden, just dig a hole sufficient for the pot and cover over with a light layer of bark. This will hide the pot and make it look as if the plant has been there since the garden was started!

Clay or hypertufa pots, on the other hand, are used for their weight, as the heavier pots are much less likely to tip over in the wind. Bromeliads can be very top heavy, particularly the vase types with litres of water in the cup and surrounding leaf bases. The beauty of these pots is they age so well, giving an air of permanence to the planting.

Hanging baskets are well suited to many bromeliad species, as they tend to be much more resistant to neglect than many plants commonly used in hanging baskets. Bromeliads with hanging flower spikes, such as *Aechmea* 'Red Wine', *A. racinae*, *Billbergia* 'Windii' or *Vriesea simplex*, are ideal, as the height of the basket shows off the hanging flowers perfectly.

The more epiphytic bromeliads can be grown in perforated plastic baskets or wooden slat baskets like those used for orchids for extra air circulation.

The stoloniferous types also work well in hanging baskets. Good examples are *Cryptanthus* 'Cascade' and *Quesnelia liboniana*, as their stolons will clamber over the sides of the baskets, creating a lovely cascading effect.

Bromeliads can look excellent in communities of different species in one large pot, for example, a large aechmea underplanted with *Cryptanthus* or *Orthophytum*. Or a collection of *Vriesea* hybrids gives a riot of colour for many months. However, the golden rule for mixing bromeliads is to make sure they all like the same light levels.

When selecting pots, the most important thing to look out for is their drainage ability. Avoid pots with just one hole in the middle, or use stones above the hole to keep it free draining. Poor drainage will inevitably lead to root death and poor performing plants.

Avoid planting the bromeliad too deeply when repotting. As a generalisation, the potting mix should not come up higher than 1–2 cm above the base of the plant. Planting too deep will lead to root or vase rot. Too shallow though and the plants may never become sufficiently stabilised to set up a good root system.

ACANTHOSTACHYS

A tiny genus of only two species, of which only *Acanthostachys strobilacea* is really worth growing.

Acanthostachys strobilacea

This easy-care small plant is a cute one, with tiny yellow and red pineapples that appear just before the southern hemisphere Christmas above curious wiry silvery green leaves that tinge red in full sun. This plant has very long-lasting colour and needs high light levels so can be grown successfully on balconies, in hanging baskets or in the garden. Will eventually form a low-growing mass of foliage. A tough, wiry plant suitable for exposed sites, it can be grown in a wide range of soil types.

Below: *Acanthostachys strobilacea* has taken well as an epiphyte on this *Trachycarpus* trunk.

AECHMEA

Members of this genus can be found throughout Central and South America and in a huge range of habitats. As a result, it is wise not to generalise about their requirements, as they will vary according to where they originated. For example, aechmeas from coastal or mountainous areas of Argentina, Brazil, Bolivia and Chile are usually more cold hardy than those from tropical areas such as Central America, the Caribbean and the Amazon region.

Aechmeas contain many tank-type epiphytes, although most are also quite happy growing in a pot or in the soil. There is a huge range of foliage colours, patterns and forms, from soft greens and reds through to spiky silvers and spiny-edged maroons. The flowers are usually spectacular, often with several different colours on each spike. Some flowers will keep their colour only a few weeks, but others will last for six months or more. Often very colourful berries develop after the flowers have faded, all of which are edible. Much hybridising has been carried out within this genus and consequently there are many beautiful hybrids available from nurseries.

Above: The flower spike of *Aechmea fasciata* is very distinctive.

Top: *Aechmea allenii* growing in an environment very close to its natural habitat. Above: A bed of *Aechmea apocalyptica* makes a colourful display over winter.

Aechmea allenii

A moderately large species with broad green leaves forming an open rosette up to 45 cm in diameter. The flower spike has large bracts of baby pink and a cluster of frosted berries tipped with pink petals. It is native to tropical cloud forests, it is quite cold sensitive so best grown in a greenhouse or tropical garden.

Aechmea 'Ann Vincent'

This large plant, up to 60 cm high, is a hybrid of two large species, *A. calyculata* and *A. caudata*. It has broad dusty green leaves with blueish tips and bases,

slightly tinged with rose. The huge flower spike reaches up to 1 m tall, with a brilliant head of bright yellow and orange. Excellent for landscaping in areas with dappled light.

Aechmea apocalyptica

The combination of royal blue and vibrant orange flowers on this small aechmea really look like flames of the apocalypse. Dark olive-green leaves form a small upright rosette about 15 cm high and wide. Very hardy and able to withstand salt spray, wind and light frosts. Excellent in trees, or as a groundcover.

There is a gorgeous cultivar of *A. apocalyptica* called 'Apocalypse Now', which is not commonly available but definitely worth trying to get. It has orange-red bracts and bright yellow flowers.

Aechmea apocalyptica x gamosepala

A lovely plant suitable for mass planting. Olive-green leaves form a small upright rosette about 30 cm high and 15 cm wide. Colourful light red bracts with baby blue flowers appear over winter; after flowering, long-lasting berries of baby pink develop. Quite a tough plant, handling salt spray with ease and light frosts. Prefers shade or semi-shade.

Aechmea aquilega

A large bromeliad up to 80 cm across, with broad olive-green leaves that take on a rosy hue in strong light, shading to deep purple in full sun. The flower spike is spectacular, rising to nearly 1 m tall, with large red bracts and bright yellow flowers. Very variable, with cultivars that come in a variety of colours. It is a tough plant, but is sensitive to cold, so suitable for conservatories or indoors, or, for those lucky enough to have a genuine subtropical climate, as feature plants in lightly shaded gardens.

Aechmea araneosa

Numerous glossy green leaves with spiked edges form an attractive medium-sized rosette of up to 60 cm in diameter. The tall branched flower spike is orange red, topped with yellow flowers. This very free-flowering plant can cope with a range of light levels, from full shade to full sun, with plant appearance changing accordingly.

Aechmea 'Bert'

An old but beautiful hybrid of A. *orlandiana* and A. *fosteriana*, with the best features of both. It has tough, heavily spined, leathery leaves with black zigzag patterning over light green and a flower spike of red bracts and bright yellow petals. Although the plant appears very tough, it is rather frost sensitive. Full sun is best for leaf colour; will do very well as an epiphyte. Faster growing than A. *orlandiana*.

Aechmea biflora

A medium-sized plant with thin light green leaves edged with black curved spines. At flowering all the centre leaves turn a stunning fire-engine red, topped with a pineapple-shaped, bright yellow flowerhead. The red leaves gradually fade to orange as the plants mature. A tough customer that can handle a range of conditions, although it prefers heat and humidity.

Aechmea 'Big Stuff'

A well-shaped hybrid with glossy leaves, green on top and luscious burgundy underneath, very similar to A. 'Royal Wine', but as the name suggests, this can become quite large, with individual plants reaching a span of 50 cm. The tall flower spike carries purplish blue flowers, followed by long-lasting red berries. Best in deep shade to keep the lustrous colour of the leaves, but not very cold hardy.

Above: *Aechmea blanchetiana* will turn more vibrant orange than this photo shows, but needs full sun to do so.

Aechmea 'Black Jack'

A fairly slow-growing plant with a narrow rosette up to 30 cm high, with only a few quite thin leaves that are glossy, deep dark burgundy, almost black in colour. It has a pendulous spike of deep red berries tipped with purple petals. Ideal for deep shade, which will accentuate the dark colour, and perfect as a foil for light green leaves of other species.

Aechmea blanchetiana

A large and imposing bromeliad from the sandy soils of coastal Brazil, which was frequently used by the famous Brazilian landscaper, Roberto Burle Marx. It can reach a span of over 1 m, and has glossy green leaves that turn bronze, almost orange in high light. The branched, feathery yellow and red flower spike reaches up to 2 m high. Excellent as a feature plant in sunny, rocky landscapes or near the beach in exposed locations. Will cope with some shade, but leaf colour may stay green.

Aechmea bromeliifolia

This is quite a variable species in shape and size, and is widespread across South America. Most of the commercially available types are larger plants, up to 80 cm high, with tight cylindrical rosettes which look similar to some billbergia. The pine cone-like head of flowers is quite striking, with large red bracts on the flower stalk. Very tough plants that can handle frosts, salt spray and drought with ease. Can be grown as an epiphyte or in the soil.

Aechmea 'Burgundy'

An absolutely stunning aechmea with an impressive rosette growing approximately 70 cm across, and shiny, deep burgundy leaves, furnished with spines on the edge. The flower spike is unusual, consisting of burgundy berries tipped with white. Colour holds

well in shade, but is best grown in good light, avoiding the midday sun. Reasonably hardy.

Aechmea caesia

Medium-sized rosette of green leaves dusted with white, and serrated with black on the edges. The rosette is very attractively shaped, being broader at the bottom and narrow at the top. The flower spike is like an open version of A. fasciata.

Aechmea callichroma

Another large and imposing bromeliad that can reach a height of over 1 m when in flower. It has olive-green leaves with a slight bronze tinge in high light. The branched, feathery flower spike has a pale pink stem and bracts, with yellow flower bracts tipped with yellow petals clustered at the end of each branch. Excellent plants for featuring among rocks and on banks where they can stand out.

Aechmea calyculata

This small plant has light green leaves tinged with lilac in high light. Cute little flower tufts of bright yellow and red sit on 30–50 cm stems. A tough aechmea that is adaptable to most situations, with cheerful flowers to brighten up most gardens.

Aechmea candida

A medium-sized rosette up to 60 cm in diameter, with green leaves covered with grey scales. The flower spike is unusual in that it is covered with a white woolly substance; the flowers themselves are pale pink with white petals, all of which, except the petals, are covered in the wool.

Left: The tough, spiky tubes of *Aechmea bromeliifolia* develop near flowering.

Aechmea caudata

This species has stiff grey-green leaves tinged with blue on the tips, which form a slender upright vase that can reach 1 m high. Reddish bracts and lime-yellow florets appear on a 1 m tall, branched flower stem, giving the distinct impression from a distance that the flower spike is a deep orange. In full sun the leaves turn a golden green which can be quite attractive. It is very vigorous, so should be planted where it can dominate an area without fear of overgrowing slower varieties. Irregular thick stripes of pale yellow or cream can arise on some offshoots, but this variegation is not stable from generation to generation. A very hardy plant, able to withstand salt spray, frost and wind.

The variety A. *caudata* var. *variegata* is much slower growing, but very attractive with thin stripes of cream down each leaf which are quite stable.

Top: The bright little tuft of *Aechmea calyculata*.
Above: *Aechmea caudata* in full flower.

Aechmea chantinii

It is almost impossible to resist buying one of these outstanding plants when they come into the garden centres, but be aware that they are very cold sensitive, with leaf damage occurring below 10°C and once temperatures drop below 5°C they usually die. Best for the greenhouse or tropical gardens. The olive-green leaves are regularly patterned with thick bands of silver, making this a striking plant in or out of flower. The flower spike has large drooping bracts of red, with a branched cluster of red and yellow flowers at the top.

This is a favoured plant of breeders for the house-plant market and there are many hybrids and cultivars. Most, however, suffer from the poor cold resistance of the parent. A. chantinii 'Samurai' is a particularly spectacular cultivar, with its green, silver-banded leaves, with bold creamy white, almost yellow stripes up the centre. The cultivar A. chantinii 'Shogun' has the variegation on the leaf margins and the flower spike has more red than the comparatively orange-looking 'Samurai'.

Aechmea coelestis

This species has olive-green leaves that are quite tough. The pink bracts and stem of the pyramidal flower spike are covered in a white fuzz, giving it a most curious appearance; light baby-blue petals appear from the tips. After flowering, jet-black berries form, often with seed in them; the berries can stay on the plant for some months. This aechmea can withstand light frosts.

There is also a variegated form with creamy white stripes down each side of the leaves, called A. coelestis var. albomarginata.

Aechmea colombiana

A large aechmea with long thin dark green leaves which form a low, sparse and spreading rosette up to 1 m in diameter. The club-like flower spike has large bracts of lilac or soft red from which the white-petalled flowers peek. A native to the Amazonian forests of Colombia, so it is quite cold sensitive and best grown in a greenhouse or tropical garden.

Aechmea correia-araujoi

The strong zigzag banding of dark brown over green make this a handsome species. The branched flower spike is quite drab in comparison to the spectacular foliage, with a few red bracts and greenish yellow flowers. The pups arise on thick strong stolons, great for planting as an epiphyte or in hanging baskets where the unusual foliage can be best seen.

Aechmea 'Covata'

This excellent landscape or patio plant is very adaptable, and forms a fast-growing and dense clump of medium-sized, spiky rosettes which look great scrambling over volcanic rocks. It produces long dark green leaves in deep shade, and short grey-green leaves in full sun. Large torch-like flowerheads of red and yellow appear on short stems in late spring to mid-summer. A very tough plant that can take salt spray, frost and wind with ease.

Aechmea cylindrata

This species forms a medium-sized upright rosette up to 50 cm high. It has deep green leaves, which get a tinge of red in high light conditions. It has pink and blue flowers from late spring to summer. Quite vigorous and so is good where a quick groundcover is needed; excellent under dense trees or in ferneries.

This page, above: This form of *Aechmea colombiana* has a lovely shade of lilac on the flower bracts.

Opposite, top: As if the beautiful leaves weren't enough, *Aechmea chantinii* shows off its glorious flower spike. Bottom: After flowering, *Aechmea coelestis* forms these lush black berries.

A. 'Blue Ice' is a selection made at Exotica nursery, and is a definite improvement on this species, with ice-blue petals over frosty white bracts.

Aechmea dealbata

A beautiful bromeliad, with purplish undersides to the leaves, which are banded with silver; the upper surface is green, forming a nice contrast. The growth habit is upright and stiff, making it a good feature plant. The flower spike looks like A. *fasciata*, but is heavily dusted with silver and the petals are red instead of blue.

Aechmea dichlamydea var. trinitensis

One of the most outstanding members of the *Aechmea* genus, this plant reaches 1 m in width and height. The massive branched, arching flower spike carries many vivid blue florets, which flower over a period of several months; the vivid pink stem sets off the florets beautifully. Can be grown in semi-shade, but is frost sensitive.

This page, top: *Aechmea 'Exotica Mystique'* has a grand appearance. Above: *Aechmea distichantha* fits in well with a stark combination of rocks and grasses.

Opposite, top: *Aechmea fasciata purpurea* foliage is shaded green when grown in shade, but deep maroon purple if grown in more sun.
Bottom: *Aechmea fasciata 'Silver King'* has heavily silvered foliage.

Aechmea distichantha

Large, spiky plants up to 1.5 m high when in flower. Not for the faint-hearted, with its silver-grey leaves with needle-sharp terminal spines and strongly serrated edges. The stunning flower spike of rose-pink bracts tipped with blue to purple flower petals can be seen for some distance and last for months. A very tough plant that can handle cold, salt spray, wind and drought and still grow well.

The variety A. *distichantha* var. *glaziovii* is a lovely plant, with a medium-sized rosette of dark green leaves, lightly banded with silver on the undersides. The flower spike is soft pink, with purple flower petals. Much smaller than the other A. *distichantha* varieties and less heavily spined.

Aechmea 'Exotica Mystique'

A dramatic hybrid, unique to the Exotica nursery where it was bred. Large plants more than 1 m high and over 1.5 m wide. In high light the rich red leaves turn a deep maroon, almost purple, with irregular concentric bands of deeper purple. The flower spike reaches up to 1 m high and has large stem bracts the same colour as the plant; the flower clusters are arranged on the top half of the flower spike and consist of bright yellow waxy-looking clumps, from which the tiny orange petals appear. This plant needs a warm spot but full sun bleaches the colour out of the leaves, so it is best in strong but dappled light. It probably won't handle direct frost on the leaves given its parentage of A. *aquilega* and A. *lueddemanniana* 'Rubra'. Ideal for conservatories and indoor planting.

Aechmea fasciata

This stunning landscape and house plant was brought to Europe in 1826 and has since been keenly sought after. Originally from Rio de Janeiro, this plant and many hybrids are now grown worldwide in the millions. The plant is a classic vase shape, very pleasing to the eye, in broad leaves of dark green, with silver-white bands. Even without a flower this is a striking plant, but when it flowers, it is a show-stopper. The pyramidal flowerhead is raised about 15 cm above the vase and has spiky, shocking-pink flower bracts and blue flower petals, a sumptuous combination. Brilliant as a potted plant, an epiphyte, or groundcover under light shade.

Of the many hybrids and varieties now available, A. *fasciata* 'Morgana' is one of the more vigorous cultivars and is more silvered than the original species.

A. *fasciata purpurea* is a selection with dark purple leaves, and is smaller than the species. A lovely cultivar of this, 'Kiwi', has purple leaves heavily striped in green, with very light silver cross banding. The variety 'Silver King' has green leaves heavily dusted with silver, creating an overall silver-grey appearance.

A. *fasciata* 'Albomarginata' has white leaf margins.

Aechmea fendleri

This plant has a large rosette of green leaves with a slight silver tinge, up to 70 cm across. It has an impressive brush of lavender-coloured flowers on a pink stem dusted with a white bloom, which can reach 1 m in height; the flowering display lasts several weeks, followed by delightful blue berries. A lovely plant for dappled light.

Aechmea 'Fosters Favorite'

This glamorous hybrid has glossy foliage, dark burgundy on both sides of the leaves. In higher light tinges of green will appear, and the long-lasting dark berries held on a pendulous stem are an added bonus. Ideal as an epiphyte particularly in tree ferns.

Aechmea 'Fosters Favorite Favorite'

This plant has glorious glossy, rose-coloured leaves with cream margins and a green to wine-red central stripe depending on light levels, and produces long-lasting orange-red berries. An awesome house plant or for warm well-sheltered gardens. Quite frost sensitive and needs bright light but no direct sunlight. Very slow growing but well worth the wait.

Aechmea gamosepala

One of the first aechmeas I grew and still one of my favourites. If grown in full shade with plenty of nutrients, it will develop dark, glossy, arching green leaves which can reach 70 cm in height. In bright light or low-nutrient situations the leaves turn a light green to almost gold colour, and usually grow more

Top left: One of the most sumptuous, but tender bromeliads, *Aechmea* 'Fosters Favorite Favorite'.
Left: The tall flower spike of *Aechmea gamosepala* always attracts attention.

erect to about 40–50 cm high. In either case, this plant is a dependable bloomer, with the first flower spikes appearing in late autumn and the last fading in late winter. Once the distinctive blue and pink bottlebrush-shaped spikes have finished flowering, the spike turns dark pink and stays in colour till mid-summer. The plant holds its pups close to the mother plant, so once established the clump forms an effective groundcover. One plant will produce 2–5 pups per year, with the clump typically doubling in area each year. It is best for slightly shady areas where the foliage keeps its best colour and the flowers really stand out. It is relatively hardy, so can be grown outdoors in areas which receive only mild frosts. It is easy to use as an epiphyte or as a pot plant inside.

A. *gamosepala* var. *nivea* has similar shape and leaf colour to the species, but with pink-red bracts and cream petals. A. 'Cappuccino' is a selection of A. *gamosepala* var. *nivea* made at Exotica nursery, with quite an unusual colour combination of chocolate brown with creamy white petals. The variety A. *gamosepala* 'Lucky Stripe' has striking stripes of cream running up the leaves. The variegation varies from plant to plant: some plants have only a single stripe down each side while others are so heavily striped as to appear almost white.

Above: The cream and pink flower spikes of *Aechmea gamosepala* var. *nivea*.

Aechmea kertesziae

Slightly more grey-coloured foliage than A. *gamosepala*, but otherwise similar in appearance. Reddish bracts and bright yellow petals show up well from a distance. After flowering, the flower spike turns an unusual brick-red colour that lasts for months. A good tough groundcover plant which flowers reliably in spring.

Aechmea 'Little Harve'

A stunning hybrid of A. *chantinii* which grows to a reasonably large rosette of green leaves with a silver dusting. The leaves blush red under high light levels. It has imposing flowers with large pink-red scape bracts and orange-yellow flowers. Quite sensitive to cool conditions, so best in subtropical gardens or indoors. Fairly slow growing.

Top left: An *Aechmea lueddemanniana* 'Rubra' flower.
Top right: *Aechmea lueddemanniana* 'Mend' is attractive even without its flowers.
Above: *Aechmea mexicana*.

Aechmea lueddemanniana

A large stately plant with up to 1 m spread, and olive-green foliage with rosy tinges in good light. The stunning flower spike has lavender-petalled flowers which develop into white berries that last for several months, gradually turning purple and creating a beautiful effect of purple and white. Full sun may cause some scorching, so it is best in dappled light; is slightly frost sensitive. It looks good as a pot plant or accent plant in the landscape.

The cultivar 'Rubra' has leaves which turn a lovely maroon colour in strong light, and is more tolerant of direct sunlight. The cultivar 'Mend' has beautiful wide stripes of cream down each side of the leaves, which turn pink in bright light, and can also tolerate full sun, if acclimatised first. *A. lueddemanniana* 'Alvarez' is also beautifully variegated with a broad stripe of creamy gold up the centre of each leaf.

Aechmea mexicana

One of the larger aechmeas which looks great in pots or as an accent plant in the garden. Light grey-green leaves have a rose colouration in bright light. The tall flower stalk has rose-coloured flowers followed by very long-lasting and gorgeous white berries. As the leaves are quite thin this plant needs a sheltered and frost-free position to look its best.

Aechmea nudicaulis

This is one of the most widespread bromeliads in the Americas, found in almost every region, usually as an epiphyte. It is a tough tubular plant with prominent spines bordering mottled green leaves. Cylindrical upright, fire-engine red and yellow spikes in mid- to late summer are clearly visible from a distance of at least 20 m. It can take relatively harsh conditions, and doesn't have much root system when grown in soil, so is best grown as an epiphyte or over rocks, and looks spectacular placed in trees.

The variety A. *nudicaulis* var. *cuspidata* is also a spectacular plant for placing in trees. The black leaf edge spines are more prominent than in the species, and the flower stem is more open and hangs slightly. A. *nudicaulis* 'Mary Hyde' is similar to the other A. *nudicaulis* varieties in flower appearance and plant shape, but with cream variegated leaf margins. A dramatic plant which looks great planted on tree fern walls or nestled in trees. A. *nudicaulis* var. *aequalis* is a beautiful plant with reddish green leaves that are banded in silver underneath.

Top right: The berries of *Aechmea mexicana* are almost pearl-like in their translucence.
Right: The very beautiful flower spike of *Aechmea nudicaulis*.

Aechmea orlandiana

Discovered in 1939 by the great bromeliad collector Mulford Foster, this species has never been found again in its native habitat. Fortunately, it is now widespread due to its bizarre beauty which appeals to enthusiasts the world over. *A. orlandiana* has tough, heavily spined, leathery leaves which are wavy in appearance. The patterning is superb, with zigzags and spots of deep maroon and black over light green leaves. The flower spike consists of red bracts and bright yellow petals, which gradually turn into purple berries. Although the plant appears very tough, it is rather frost sensitive. Full sun is best for leaf colour and these plants do very well as an epiphyte; it is very slow growing.

The variety 'Ensign' is notable for its beautiful stripes of white on the edge of the leaves, which take on a pink hue in full sun. The cultivar commonly known as 'Reverse Ensign' has variegated leaves with the variegation in the middle of the leaf and green margins.

Aechmea pectinata

These stunning plants can reach over 1 m wide. The mottled green leaves are liberally splashed with vibrant pink and the leaves turn this pink colour from the tips to nearly the base at flowering. Great as a focus plant in a tropical landscape, it also looks spectacular in the top of an old tree fern stump. Try not to shift it once it shows leaf colour, as the pink parts will likely fade to pale green, with pink appearing in other areas, detracting from its appearance.

Aechmea phanerophlebia

A large imposing vase-shaped rosette of silver- and green-banded leaves that are quite heavily spined; it reaches a height and spread of 50 cm as a single plant. The outer leaves curve down, while the inner leaves form a tube which supports the dramatic flower spike. The spike consists of many spiky rose-pink to red bracts, which last for months in colour. A striking plant for landscaping with rocks and succulents or on a balcony in full sun, it is relatively slow growing.

Aechmea pineliana var. minuta

This gorgeous plant has stiff spiky leaves with shades of bronze, pink and copper, lightly barred with silver on the underside when grown in full sun. Bright red flower stalks appear in winter, topped with bottlebrush-like flowers in yellow, fading to black. A very tough plant that can withstand frost, full sun and salt spray, it is perfect for rocky gardens.

Aechmea 'Pink Rocket'

A lovely hybrid of A. *fendleri* and A. *fasciata*, with the best of both species. In high light the leaves take on a beautiful pink colour, overlaid with silver; in shade, this colour is lost completely, to green leaves overlaid with silver. It has a similar flower spike to A. *fasciata*, but is more elongated and with rosy pink, almost red bracts topped with purple flowers.

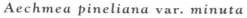

This page, top left: Aechmea 'Pink Rocket'. Top right: *Aechmea phanerophlebia* growing well in this macadamia. Right: Splashes of shocking pink from this *Aechmea pectinata* in flower.

Opposite, left: Aechmea orlandiana with the light shining through the leaves. Right: *Aechmea orlandiana* 'Ensign'.

Top: The leaves of *Aechmea* 'Red Wine' always have a glossy lustre. Above: *Aechmea recurvata* var. *benrathii* forms spiky but colourful clusters.

Aechmea racinae

A pretty little plant with small rosettes of glossy light green leaves. The lovely little berry-like red and yellow flowers hang down from the plants, making this ideal for hanging baskets or planted as an epiphyte in the garden. Flowering time is mid-winter, Christmas in the northern hemisphere, hence its common name of 'Christmas Jewel'.

Aechmea ramosa

A very fine and large aechmea with many narrow, shiny green leaves forming a rosette that can grow up to 75 cm wide. The branched flower spike has red bracts and stem, with light yellow flowers. After the relatively short flowering period, a mass of yellow berries form, which are very long lasting; the weight of the berries can be so much that the previously upright stem becomes pendant. It is reasonably cold hardy. There is also a red-leaved form which is quite stunning but difficult to obtain.

Aechmea recurvata

This species and its varieties all come from Brazil, where they are found on trees and over rock formations. The whole plant appears to have been spray-painted bright red when in flower, and is quite spectacular, particularly on host trees. The flower of *A. recurvata* var. *recurvata* protrudes above the foliage more than the other varieties. They all look great on driftwood or tree fern slabs and are also stylish in rock gardens. All *A. recurvata* hybrids are very tough, able to withstand salt spray, wind and some frost.

The variety *A. recurvata* var. *benrathii* is a gorgeous little gem with little spiky rosettes of grey foliage that turn bright pink to red at flowering; the bright pink flowers are held low.

A. recurvata var. *ortgiesii* has hard, spiny, grey-green foliage which turns bright orange to red at flowering; and bright purple or pink flowers held low in the vase. One of the cultivars of *A. recurvata* includes 'Aztec Gold' which is a lovely variegated plant with golden yellow variegations.

Aechmea 'Red Bands'

This older hybrid of *A. triangularis*, and possibly

A. maculata, is very striking with upright tubular rosettes of nicely tapered and arching spiny leaves. The colour changes from light green in shade to gold in full sun, always with heavy rusty red banding. It is very hardy and able to handle most conditions.

Aechmea 'Red Wine'

Rich maroon colouring on both sides of the leaves makes this a beautiful plant for deep shade. Try underplanting with a green groundcover such as moss to highlight the deep colouration. Avoid high light, as this will wash the colouring out, leaving pale green, stressed-looking leaves. The beautiful upright cluster of deep red berries tipped with deep purple petals makes a stunning sight in summer.

Aechmea 'Royal Wine'

This gracious plant has glossy dark green foliage with dark maroon undersides. It always looks glamorous and the long-lasting berries are an added bonus. It also makes an excellent house plant, being tolerant of low light conditions. This was the first bromeliad I ever grew after being given one by my grandmother, and it is still growing 25 years later.

Aechmea serrata

A lovely aechmea with a very good shape that reaches approximately 75 cm across and high, and has shiny green leaves that are quite spiky on the edges. The flower spike is both very imposing and pretty, with a pineapple-like head of translucent pearl and lilac bracts; the flower remains in colour for some months. It makes a good feature plant in the garden.

Aechmea spectabilis

A large and impressive plant with a rosette that can reach more than 1 m in width. It has glossy green

Above: *Aechmea* 'Royal Wine' has pendant spikes of long-lasting berries.

leaves that turn apricot in strong light. The multiple-branched flower stem reaches more than 1 m in height and is comprised of many berry-like pink flowers tipped with red petals. It is quite frost sensitive, but makes a dramatic statement in sub-tropical or tropical gardens, or in conservatories and well-lit windows in cooler climates.

Aechmea triangularis

This plant has stiff upright rosettes of spiky dark green leaves. A curiosity of this species is the curled-down leaf tips, which are a distinguishing feature. The cone-shaped flower spikes with dark violet flowers and fire-engine red stem bracts are beautiful. It is quite tough and able to handle frosts, salt spray, drought and wind with ease. Excellent as epiphytes or over rocks, but also happy planted in the soil.

Aechmea triticina

A commonly grown species, which is possibly misnamed, with stiff upright rosettes of spiky green leaves. The cone-shaped flower spikes with lemon-yellow flowers and red stem bracts are best described as curious rather than beautiful. Very hardy plants that can handle a wide range of conditions, including full sun and drought; also very prolific, so useful for covering large areas quickly.

The variety A. *triticina* var. *capensis* has bronze leaves that tinge orange-red in full sun. The flowerhead looks even more like a bottlebrush than the species, with thin yellow bracts covering it like hair.

Aechmea warasii

This plant has soft leaves of copper red lightly tinged with green. It has a pendulous flower stalk with fat red berries tipped with white-edged lavender petals; the flower stalk usually hangs lower than the plant, making it perfect for growing as an epiphyte in shady gardens, or in a hanging basket inside.

Aechmea weilbachii

This species has soft, very glossy, light green leaves, which form an attractive vase of up to 70 cm high and wide. Beautiful flowers of lilac purple, which

look like berries, are held on top of brilliant red bracts and a stem of 60–80 cm. It is quite slow to flower, so may need a hurry along with ethylene from time to time (see page 180). Reasonably hardy, but best in warm gardens where there is dappled light or full shade.

Aechmea winkleri

A relatively small, well-shaped rosette of green leaves tinged with purple at the tips. The bright red flower stem tipped with yellow flowers looks like a miniature Christmas tree. The flower spike stays this colour for many weeks, eventually turning dark red and lasting for several months. Quite hardy and able to adjust from full shade to nearly full sun if given sufficient time to acclimatise.

Above left: This close-up shows the lovely copper colouring of *Aechmea warasii*. Below: *Aechmea winkleri*.

ALCANTAREA

This genus has been recently split off the *Vriesea*
genus. It contains 17 species, all from eastern Brazil
and mostly very large plants. They are typically
found perched on rocky cliffs, so require very free
draining soil. Alcantareas are quite adaptable from
shade to full sun, but usually develop their best
colour and shape in full sun or very light shade.
Although they may appear very tropical, in fact most
of them can handle at least light frosts, with some
able to take fairly heavy frosts.

Alcantarea geniculata

Only brought into cultivation in the late 1990s from Brazil, this large species reaches a span of about 1 m across, with wide, glossy green leaves. The flower spike reaches 1 m high, with deep pink bracts and creamy yellow branches. Although still relatively rare in cultivation, it is very sought after for its size and beauty so more plants are now becoming available. Although the glossy green leaves would suggest otherwise, this plant can be acclimatised to cope with full sun or shade. Reasonably frost hardy and able to cope with wind and salt spray.

Alcantarea imperialis

One of the giant bromeliads, this grows to a span of more than 1.5 m, although it takes up to 10 years to reach this size. The slightly ribbed leaves are quite leathery and tough with a distinctive waxy bloom over the surface, which gives a bluish appearance from a distance. The thick flower spike reaches up to 2.5 m in height, producing hundreds of slightly fragrant white flowers. The plant can withstand relatively cool nights as it is native to mountains near Rio de Janeiro at an elevation of about 1500 m.

The variety A. imperialis 'Rubra' is particularly sought after, for the deep red cast the leaves take on in full sun. A. imperialis 'Purple' is another highly sought-after form, but is much more difficult to obtain. It has deep burgundy to purple leaves.

Alcantarea odorata

This alcantarea is slightly smaller than many of the others in this genus, at less than 1 m in diameter, making it more suitable for smaller gardens. The rosette is comprised of many slender green leaves, faintly banded in silver, which finish in thin graceful

arching tips. The leaves are covered with a white waxy powder, which gives the plant an overall blue look. The flower spike is stunning with red bracts and fragrant flowers.

Alcantarea vinicolor

Still quite rare in cultivation, but should become more widely available soon as commercial nurseries rush to grow these lovely plants. Native to Espirito Santo, Brazil, these plants can take up to 15 years to come into flower, by which time it may be up to 1.5 m high and wide. The branched flower spike reaches approximately 2.5 m high, and carries many flowers with pale peach petals. The plant is very similar in appearance to A. imperialis 'Rubra', but is smaller and with much more intense, burgundy-red colouring.

This page, above: *Alcantarea vinicolor* among tropical flowers and foliage.

Opposite, top left: *Alcantarea geniculata*. Top right: *Alcantarea imperialis* has stiff thick leaves, which are very hardy. Bottom: A mature *Alcantarea imperialis* 'Rubra' with a height and span of approximately 1.5 m.

ANANAS

This genus contains less than 10 species, most of which are quite large and need warm climates to succeed, and includes the classic bromeliad of commerce, the pineapple.

Ananas bracteatus

This species is native to coastal areas of Brazil, and needs full sun to develop the intense red colouration on the spiky leaves. At flowering, a bright red pineapple forms, which is initially surrounded by a ring of brilliant blue petals.

The variegated form of this species, A. *bracteatus* var. *tricolor* is a riot of colour, but needs high light levels to bring out the best colour.

Ananas comosus

The original species of A. *comosus* has relatively small fruit, about 15–20 cm high. It also has exceptionally spiky leaves, with the result that few people now grow this plant.

The variety 'Smooth Cayenne' is the main pineapple variety grown. Rosettes of up to 1 m wide consisting of smooth grey-green leaves make this a much easier plant to deal with than the original species. It is very attractive, particularly when in fruit; leave the fruit on the plant until it changes colour to yellow-orange and you will have a taste sensation that will make you wonder where the true pineapple taste has gone in commercially grown fruit.

A. *comosus* 'Sugar Loaf' is a slightly smaller plant than 'Smooth Cayenne' and is very good for the home garden as it produces extremely sweet juicy fruit.

The variety *A. comosus* var. *variegatus* is a spectacular plant. The variegated leaves have thick stripes of ivory white down each edge, and in high light levels the edge spines are coloured pink, which is also the colour the inner leaves turn at flowering. The fruit starts out as bright red.

Ananas nanus

This little species is sometimes available as plants, but can also be purchased from florists who use the cute little pineapples in flower arrangements. The tops of these can be grown on like the commercial pineapple. It has arching, 30–45 cm, reasonably spiky, grey-green leaves. The flower spike reaches up to 60 cm and has reddish buds which open into purple flowers. By the time it reaches the florist it has formed a 5 cm-long, fragrant, edible pineapple.

This page, top right: *Ananas bracteatus* var. *tricolor* in an open woodland setting.
Right: *Ananas bracteatus* in fruit.

Opposite, top: *Ananas comosus* 'Smooth Cayenne' in fruit.
Bottom: *Ananas comosus* var. *variegatus* can get a bit strappy in shady gardens.

BILLBERGIA

Billbergia are so widespread and common in cultivation that people are often surprised to find they are bromeliads. The comment is usually: 'Oh, my grandmother had these in her garden.' The *Billbergia* genus contains about 60 species, and is comprised of tank-type epiphytes, which can also grow in the soil. These plants are distinctive for having relatively few leaves, arranged in tall cylinders or slender vases, often barred with silver or maroon, or spotted with cream or pink. The flower spikes are most often pendulous, sometimes hanging below the base of the plant and are usually very glamorous. Although striking in flower, the flowering season is usually very short, sometimes only a couple of weeks.

Billbergia are all quite prolific and can naturalise and take over an area within a few short years. For this reason it is often advisable to grow them as nature intended — in trees, which stops them from becoming a nuisance and has the added side benefit of producing more highly coloured foliage as well as offering better visibility of the flowers.

Some species, such as *Billbergia nutans*, *B. vittata* and *B. zebrina* are very tough, able to withstand high winds, full sun, extended droughts and salt spray. Others like *B. pyramidalis* are quite tender and will suffer in direct sun, cold or drought.

This page, above: *Billbergia amoena* 'Red'.

Opposite: A young plant of *Billbergia brasiliensis* already showing the distinctive silver banding.

Billbergia amoena

A fairly large and attractive billbergia with pink and spotted cream leaves when grown in good light. The upright flower spikes have shocking pink bracts and green flowers with bright blue tips. It is very prolific and can cover large areas quite quickly via its underground stolons.

The form B. amoena var. stolonifera has slightly banded, greyish foliage, and is more suited to growing as an epiphyte, as the stolons tend to clamber and hang down. The most notable member of this species is B. amoena 'Red', which is very similar to B. amoena var. stolonifera, but has glorious glossy red leaves. The new pups arise from relatively long stolons and often grow much higher than the parent plant. This unusual characteristic means it can be grown as a climber. The upright flower spike has prominent bright red bracts.

Billbergia brasiliensis

Thin, stiff olive-green leaves, shading to bronze in full sun, form a tight tubular plant. The leaves are heavily banded with thick silver bands, particularly on the underside; even when not in flower this plant is very striking. The cascading flower stem features large pink bracts and long petals of the truest purple. Quite frost tender, but otherwise capable of withstanding the elements. Best as an epiphyte to display the banding and the long flower spike.

Billbergia 'Catherine Wilson'

A bizarre hybrid with a stiff upright tubular vase of leaves, green inside and pink with purple markings outside, heavily marbled with white. However, the inside of the leaf also appears on the outside, as the leaf tips are completely rolled over in a tight curl.

Billbergia distachia

This plant has dark green leaves in shade, which changes to a reddish green in full sun. B. distachia has several flushes of semi-pendant stems of pink bracts and green flowers throughout the year. Use this as a dense groundcover, or to climb the trunk of palms or pongas.

Billbergia 'Fantasia'

A long-established and beautiful hybrid, this has a stiff upright vase of green leaves, so heavily marbled with white as to appear almost pure white from a distance. In full sun the white areas take on a pink tinge. The scarlet flower spike has the same appearance as the B. pyramidalis parent, although opens to a looser arrangement when in full flower.

Billbergia 'Hoelscheriana'

This very old hybrid of *B. nutans* and *B. saundersii* is an exotic-looking plant, due to its tubular vase of serrated green leaves coated with white spots and tinged pink red if grown in high light. The hanging flower spikes have bright cerise bracts, with purple-tipped green flowers. It is much showier than *B. nutans* and flowers slightly later in the spring. Very hardy, able to take considerable frost, wind, drought and salt spray, it is best grown as an epiphyte.

Billbergia 'Muriel Waterman'

A justifiably famous and widely grown hybrid, with wide burgundy-coloured leaves, which take on a pink cast in full sun, banded with silver underneath the leaves; the leaf tips can be quite rolled. The flower is not as spectacular as the foliage in this hybrid. Quite tough and able to take full sun, frost and drought, it is very good as an epiphyte, but can also be grown easily as a pot plant or in the garden.

Billbergia nutans

One of the most durable bromeliads that has been around for many years, it has leaves held in a thin, upright vase. It flowers in early spring with pink hanging flowers. Often found in old abandoned gardens — testament to its toughness — it will form a very dense, weed-suppressing groundcover, or can be kept in the trees to avoid it getting out of control.

Billbergia pyramidalis

This simply stunning plant has large, wide emerald-green leaves forming a relatively open medium-sized rosette. The flowerhead looks like an Olympic torch and is most impressive; it is predominantly red with purple tips to the petals and bright yellow pollen. Ideal as a pot plant or patio plant, but also looks

This page, top: *Billbergia* 'Hoelscheriana' makes a great epiphyte.
Above: What looks to be unmown grass is in fact a mass of *Billbergia nutans*, naturalised here for decades.

Opposite, left: Although short lived, the flower of *Billbergia pyramidalis* 'Kyoto' is breathtaking.
Right: The contentious *Billbergia pyramidalis* 'Striata'.

great under subtropical shrubs. This is one of the stoloniferous billbergias and will gradually climb over any object placed next to it. Use this ability to good effect in the garden and in pots. Curiously, if planted in good soil, the climbing habit is lost completely and the plants clump in the same way as many other bromeliads; flowering may also become more prolific. It is possible that the climbing habit is simply a response to less than ideal conditions.

The cultivar 'Kyoto' is a very dramatic billbergia with emerald-green leaves with a white margin. This species and its hybrids are very cold tender, so should only be grown in the subtropics or inside. *B. pyramidalis* 'Striata' is the subject of much debate, as in all likelihood it is not a *B. pyramidalis* at all, with its quite different leaf type and hanging flower spike. It has an open rosette of dusty green leaves with heavy cream bands running down the sides. A striking plant even when not in flower, it is spectacular in flower. The yellow form *B.* 'Gloria' is a sport of 'Striata', which often arises from large old clumps.

Billbergia 'Santa Barbara'

A relatively small but very attractive billbergia, with cream and green stripes which become flushed with pink in good light. Small flower stems with pink bracts and green flowers.

Billbergia 'Theodore L. Mead'

This variety has slender tubes of grey-green leaves, but its major attraction is the relatively long-lasting flowers (for this genus). It has rose-pink bracts and blue and green flowers. It forms a dense weed-suppressing groundcover; and can take full shade to medium light.

Billbergia vittata

One of the first bromeliads introduced to the United States, it is now so extensively hybridised that it is difficult to make accurate identifications. However, the species has tubular rosettes of silver-banded leaves that take on a maroon, almost purple hue when grown in full sun. The hanging flower stem has glorious salmon-pink bracts tipped with deep purple flowers. Spectacular in flower, although short lived.

Billbergia 'Windii'

One of the oldest surviving bromeliad hybrids, this was first created in 1882, and has relatively long, wavy, dark green leaves which form an open rosette. The flowers consist of large rose-pink bracts and blue and green flowers. The flower stem often hangs down lower than the plant, so this is ideal as an epiphyte, for sitting on a bench, or planting in a hanging basket.

Billbergia zebrina

This species has tall tubes of green leaves heavily banded with silver, which develop shades of bronze in strong light. Large rose-pink bracts cover the hanging flower spike; and long greenish yellow petals make for an unusual combination. After flowering, attractive silver berries form which last for months. It is very hardy and can be grown in a wide range of light levels.

Top left: The long, drooping flowers of *Billbergia* 'Windii' emerge through the surrounding foliage.
Above: *Billbergia vittata*.

BROMELIA

This genus of approximately 50 species comes from habitats as diverse as rainforests and dry coastal areas. Most species are difficult to obtain, simply because they are so ferocious that few people grow them.

In their native lands, several of the species are used as impenetrable hedging.

Below: The traffic-stopping red of *Bromelia balansae* in full flower.

Bromelia balansae

This is a bromeliad to be treated with caution and is not for the faint hearted. Large rosettes of silvery green foliage up to 1.5 m in diameter and height are edged in vicious curved spines and tipped with near daggers. However, if you have a desert- or Mediterranean-style garden this is an essential for dry rocky areas where it can be left alone. Striking as a foliage plant only, it is stunning in flower when all the central leaves turn fiery red, topped with a felted, white flower spike with dark red and white flower petals. It is very hardy and capable of withstanding extended droughts and frosts down to -9°C.

Top left: A thorny thicket of *Bromelia pinguin*. Top right: After *Bromelia pinguin* flowers, these large, edible fruit develop. Above: A young offshoot of a *Bromelia pinguin* hybrid, with lovely orange colouring to the leaves.

Bromelia pinguin

Sometimes called the wild pineapple, *B. pinguin* does resemble the pineapple, and its fruit is edible. However, that is where the resemblance ends, as this species grows up to 2 m high, with thin, heavily spiked leaves. The flowering period is spectacular, with the central leaves turning fire-engine red, from which the felted, white flower spike with light pink flowers appears. The fruit is comprised of individual berries which look like small plums and are quite acidic. Equally as tough as *B. balansae*, but larger and much more vigorous, so is best suited to very large spaces where it can flourish at will; over time this forms an impenetrable thicket and is often used as hedging.

CANISTROPSIS

This is a newly formed genus, once part of *Nidularium*. These plants all prefer heavy shade, quickly looking stressed if they are exposed to too much light. They are ideal for indoor environments, but being quite cold hardy, are also excellent for growing in shady gardens.

Canistropsis billbergioides

This is one of the best *Canistropsis* species. When grown well it has glossy dark green foliage, forming a tidy rosette about 30 cm wide. The brightly coloured star-shaped flower spikes appear in late autumn through to late winter. The plant spreads via short stolons, which can grow along the ground or move up a support such as a tree fern trunk; one plant will produce 1–3 pups per year, so you soon have a good-sized clump to work with. *C. billbergioides* is best for shady areas, where the foliage keeps its most favourable colour and the flowers really stand out. We grow them under camellias, citrus trees, avocados, tree ferns and pittosporums, and they look great under all. All of these varieties grow well as indoor pot plants and many thousands of them are produced in Europe each year for this purpose.

Above: *Canistropsis billbergioides* 'Persimmon' flower.

All of the 10 or so cultivars of this species have been recently renamed, rather bizarrely after fruit. The most common variety in Australasia is 'Persimmon', which is bright orange. 'Citron' with its lemon-yellow bracts is much more common in the United States and Europe, and is slightly smaller and more tender than 'Persimmon'. 'Tutti Frutti' is slightly larger than 'Persimmon' and has a stunning flower which changes from burnt orange when young to a deep mulberry red as it ages. Even more beautiful is the cultivar 'Guava', which has pinkish red flower bracts. Unfortunately, this cultivar is not commonly available. The slowest growing cultivar would have to be *C. billbergioides* 'Plum' which is also one of the most striking. Small rosettes of deep 'Black Doris' plum-coloured leaves are topped with the same colour star-shaped flower spikes. The colour fades to green if any direct sunlight reaches these plants.

Canistropsis burchellii

A small plant with dusty green leaves on top and deep burgundy below. The light lavender flowers are nestled deep in the centre of the cup much like a neoregelia. Although fairly nondescript, it can be useful as a groundcover for very shady areas of the garden.

Canistropsis seidelii

Shiny green leaves form an open rosette similar to *C. billbergioides*. The flower spike has the appearance of a guzmania, with layers of star-shaped bright yellow bracts clustered up the stem. It is very beautiful in flower.

Top: The dainty but very pretty star of *Canistropsis billbergioides* 'Citron'.
Above: *Canistropsis billbergioides* 'Tutti Frutti'.

CANISTRUM

A small genus of about 10 species, all native to the Atlantic coastal forests of south-eastern Brazil. Some have very exotic-looking leaf markings which make them specially suitable as feature plants in the garden. Their colourful flower spikes, which can last for several months, are similar in appearance to *Canistropsis* or *Nidularium*.

Most canistrums are found in their natural habitat growing on rocks or in trees, but are also quite amenable to growing in soil, and as they are able to adapt to low-light situations, they are also quite suitable for indoor growing.

Canistrum lindenii

This species has large rosettes of mottled green leaves, and can reach up to 75 cm wide. The long-lasting flower spike develops into a veritable bird's nest of mauve-pink bracts surrounding the petals. Prefers more shade than some of the other members of this genus.

Canistrum seidelianum

This is probably the finest member of the genus from an ornamental point of view. The well-shaped rosettes have an extraordinary appearance with dark green leaves, heavily banded and spotted with rusty red. A basket-shaped flower spike of soft peach to orange colour is held above the foliage; pale yellow petals are nestled in the cup of this basket. They are best suited to light shade, to bring out the best colour in the leaves. These plants are reasonably tough, and able to handle light frosts.

Canistrum triangulare

Quite leathery, stiff leaves form a nice rosette for this popular species. The light green leaves are tipped with dark purple, almost black markings and edged with the same colour spines. In full sun, the leaves go a golden green and the markings cover increasingly large areas of the leaf. The flower spike is a lovely blood-orange colour, with white petals nestled in the centre. Reasonably hardy and best in very light shade, it is ideal as an epiphyte, although also looks good at ground level.

Above: *Canistrum lindenii* is ideal for underplanting in shady areas.

CRYPTANTHUS

A genus of only 50 or so species from Brazil, there are probably a thousand hybrids as these little plants have their own cult following among bromeliad fanciers.

Commonly known as the earth stars, for their flat, star-shaped appearance and terrestrial habit, these little bromeliads are very appealing. The leaves are quite succulent, with wavy and serrated edges; often they will be heavily coloured, usually in shades of pink, red, maroon and purple. They also often have a dusty appearance from the specialised leaf scales, and in some plants these are collected into silver bands across the leaf.

As terrestrials, most cryptanthus need a reasonable amount of soil around the roots. Therefore, with a few exceptions, these plants need to be grown in soil, preferably free draining and with a reasonable amount of nutrients and lots of humus. They make fantastic groundcover plants, particularly under open trees, as this is similar to their natural environment. If grown in pots, the pot should be wider than it is deep, as the root systems prefer to spread out rather than go downwards.

The majority of the types available to gardeners come from low altitudes and almost without

Above: This group of *Cryptanthus* includes a *C. zonatus* hybrid, *C. fosterianus*, *C. beuckeri* and *C. bromelioides* var. *tricolor*.

exception, these little stars need warm climates. Direct frost will usually kill them outright and cold winds will damage them severely. However, if grown under trees or shrubs, the protection of these is usually sufficient to cope with light frosts. They are fairly intolerant of dry soil, so keep them well watered for best results. Some are shade lovers, but most prefer partial sun, with a few enjoying full sun.

Cryptanthus acaulis

This small cryptanthus has flat rosettes about 6–8 cm in diameter, with wavy, succulent-looking, wide dark green leaves with a slight dusting of silver. The flowers form as a cluster of white petals in the middle and contrast well with the dark leaves. In the form C. acaulis 'Rubra', which is probably more commonly grown than C. acaulis, the leaves are a dark reddish bronze. Reasonably cold sensitive, they are ideal as indoor plants and for terrariums.

The cultivar C. acaulis 'Grace' is named after the well-known Australian bromeliad breeder, Grace Goode, and is a lovely soft green with light green variegations.

Cryptanthus beuckeri

One of the most unusual species of cryptanthus, it has been the parent of many hybrids. The rosettes grow to 15 cm wide, with peculiar paddle-shaped, olive-green leaves, overlaid with complex mottles of dark and creamy green. The species and its cultivars are all quite sensitive to cold and drought. They are best grown in shady tropical gardens with plenty of humidity, or as greenhouse or terrarium subjects. They are slow growing.

Cryptanthus bivittatus

A very popular species that was discovered as long ago as 1860 in Brazil, but like so many bromeliads it is probably now extinct in its native habitat. The original form collected is also thought to have been lost forever; however, the variety C. bivittatus var. atropurpureus is very similar.

The cultivar 'Starlight' arose as a sport of this species and has quickly become one of the most favoured. This complex-coloured plant has a faint olive-green central stripe, with olive-green leaf edges. Bordering the central stripe are stripes of progressively lighter pink with the final stripe next to the border being cream. The cultivar 'Pink Starlite' has wide, light pink edge stripes as well. C. 'Ruby' is another cultivar of this species, with ruby-red and bronze stripes. All of these plants are very striking and well worth growing.

Cryptanthus bromelioides

Wavy green leaves comprise the species; however, there are many attractive forms including red, bronze, silver and copper-red leaves. Some forms have fragrant flowers.

C. bromelioides var. tricolor, recently renamed 'Rainbow Star', is the favoured form of this species, for its lovely shiny, variegated leaves in stripes of green and pinky cream. Near the base the leaves tinge to vibrant red.

Cryptanthus 'Carnival de Rio'

A riot of colour, with shades of yellow, and mottles of green, bronze and deep burgundy, overlaid with speckles of silver. In high light, most of the colours are squeezed out with a rose overlay.

Cryptanthus 'Cascade'

One of the more interesting species, with a habit of sending its pups out on long cascading stolons. In bright light the leaves go pinky bronze, while in low light the predominant colour is green. White flowers cluster in the centre of each rosette. Excellent for hanging baskets or for placing in the top of a hollowed-out tree fern.

Cryptanthus 'Dusk'

For a cryptanthus, this plant has quite large rosettes of wide, heavily serrated leaves of copper red shading to deep burgundy in good light. An excellent groundcover, it is reasonably hardy, but won't cope with frosts.

Cryptanthus fosterianus

One of the more commonly grown species, for good reason, as it is one of the more striking. The leaves are comprised of wide edges of chocolate brown, with a thick stripe of pinkish brown in the centre. The leaves are overlaid with wavy bands of silver.

Above: The broad chocolate leaves of *Cryptanthus* 'Dusk'.

Cryptanthus 'It'

This plant has a rosette of long, slender, wavy leaves with broad central stripes of near-white in low light, shading to salmon pink in high light, edged with dark olive green.

The opposite form of this is called C. 'Ti', which has a broad central stripe in shades of green, bordered by a thin band of pink.

Cryptanthus 'Le Rey'

Somewhat similar to the cultivar C. 'Ti', except the leaves are much wider and more plentiful, giving a fuller look to the rosette.

Cryptanthus 'Red Bird'

Small rosettes of slender, wavy rose-red leaves, edged with deeper red and coated with silver underneath.

Cryptanthus sinuosus

Very wavy green leaves stacked in a spiral fashion make a multi-layered rosette. Similar to C. *acaulis* and may be very closely related. Mainly of interest for some of its cultivars and the wavy leaves which come through in most hybrids made with this species.

The cultivar 'Imposter Red' has a superb coppery red glow to its leaves.

Cryptanthus zonatus

The most recognisable cryptanthus, with small rosettes of wavy green leaves, heavily banded with silver zigzags.

The variety C. *zonatus* 'Silver' has chocolate-brown leaves banded with silver, in a similar fashion to *Orthophytum gurkenii*.

xCRYPTBERGIA

Intergeneric hybrids between *Billbergia* and *Cryptanthus*, these have the toughness of *Billbergia* coupled with the leaf colour of the *Cryptanthus*. Unfortunately they also have the nondescript flowers of the *Cryptanthus*.

Adaptable from full sun to full shade, their leaf colour alters in response to light levels. The best leaf colour is achieved with full sun in regions with less intense sunlight, or light shade where the UV intensity is too high.

xCryptbergia 'Mead'

This plant has a relatively small rosette, with the pups held close so it develops a bushy appearance over time. It has leaves of medium-green speckled with pink; and the pink markings intensify in high light levels until the whole plant is almost completely pink.

xCryptbergia 'Red Burst'

A cross between *Cryptanthus bahianus* and *Billbergia nutans*, this is a slow-growing but attractive hybrid, with a small flattish rosette of deep bronze red, which intensifies in strong light. The small flowers are quite inconspicuous. It is easy to propagate and very much at home scrambling through rocks.

Top left: xCryptbergia 'Mead' develops masses of shocking pink foliage.
Above: xCryptbergia 'Red Burst' is an adaptable plant that will keep its colour in light shade or full sun.

Top: Some of the larger *Dyckia* species can have flower spikes reaching over 1.5 m tall. Above: These *Dyckia brevifolia* combine well with other succulents.

DYCKIA

Members of this genus of more than 120 species are all very hardy plants with thick, spiky, succulent leaves. These terrestrials are often found in harsh environments and almost all come from central Brazil or southern South America.

The leaves usually have a waxy or glossy appearance, with edges of sharp spines, which are sometimes very decorative. Nearly all dyckias are clump forming and are invariably left to grow this way as they are so spiky.

Usually the flower spikes bear yellow or orange flowers, which can be quite showy. Unlike most bromeliads, the plant does not die down after flowering, as the flower spike comes from the side, rather than the centre of the rosette. Virtually all dyckias flower in spring.

Although they are quite hardy and tolerant of dry conditions, they will suffer greatly if drought conditions continue to a point where the leaves start to shrivel. In this case, frequent watering is recommended, as is soil or potting mix with more water-holding capacity than would be used for other bromeliads.

If potted, it is important to use a larger pot than normal for these plants to accommodate the larger root mass — they do much better in open soil than in pots for this reason.

Dyckia brevifolia

Spiky, shiny green leaves form rosettes approximately 10 cm high and 20 cm wide on this plant. Within a short time the generous number of pups produced results in tight clumps. It has bright orange-yellow flowers on 30 cm stems. Cold hardy and able to withstand considerable drought, so it is ideal for a rockery or cactus garden.

Dyckia 'Brittle Star'

Although difficult to obtain, this plant is well worth looking for if you are interested in succulent-type bromeliads. Thin, curved brittle-looking leaves of dark brown, almost black, contrast with amazing spines of silvery white. This plant looks exactly like the name suggests.

Dyckia cinerea

This species has short, broad, almost succulent-like grey leaves, which form a small rosette up to 30 cm wide. The flower spike is slender and topped with bright yellow flowers. This plant would look at home in any cacti or succulent garden.

Dyckia fosteriana

A brittle-looking plant, but with quite tough spiky leaves of shiny silver. It has golden flowers on thin spikes.

Dyckia fosteriana 'Bronze' has a compact rosette about 15–20 cm wide, with heavily spined bronze leaves.

Below: *Dyckia cinerea* can become quite bronzed in full sun.

Dyckia ibiramensis

An attractive dyckia with shiny apple-green leaves, dusted with grey underneath and well serrated. The branched golden yellow flower spike can reach 1 m in height.

Dyckia marnier-lapostollei

A particularly lovely dyckia with silvery leaves that almost look like they are covered in velvet. On each leaf, the serrated imprint of the younger leaf can be clearly seen, making a fascinating pattern.

If possible, the variety *D. marnier-lapostollei* var. *estevii* is even more striking. It has thinner leaves, with long curved, but relatively soft spines, that look rather like long thin, silver-bronze, venus fly-trap leaves.

Dyckia 'Naked Lady'

The only dyckia to have spineless leaves, this is often called 'Nude Lady'. The leaves are an attractive golden green when grown in full sun. It is quite hardy and can handle light frosts.

Top left: The spines on *Dyckia fosteriana* 'Bronze' contrast well with the dark leaf colour.
Above: The numerous pups of *Dyckia ibiramensis* soon form a thick spiny clump.

FASCICULARIA

This genus has only a single species, *Fascicularia bicolor*.

Fascicularia bicolor

This plant, native to Chile, has long thin, heavily serrated dark green leaves which form dense rosettes. At flowering, the centre leaves turn bright red, surrounding a dense cluster of flowers of the most striking blue, offset with bright yellow pollen. A very hardy plant, capable of surviving -7°C frosts. In their native habitat they are often found on seaside cliffs, so are ideal for rockeries and banks, where they can sprawl at will.

Below: *Fascicularia bicolor* in full bloom; this is a small form with mauve petals.

GUZMANIA

The majority of this genus of approximately 185 species are tank-type epiphytes, native to tropical rainforests where they inhabit the lower sections of the jungle. Those that grow as terrestrials, mostly the larger species, grow in the leaf mould on the jungle floor, which is close to epiphytic conditions. Therefore they all need very free-draining soil or potting mix if they are to be grown as pot plants or in the garden.

Although most of the species are not commonly grown, the hybrids have been produced in their millions by Dutch, Belgian and North American nurseries, and are now some of the most widespread houseplants in the world.

The smooth-edged leaves are usually green, although there are a few variegated and reddish coloured types and some with the intricate patterning more commonly associated with *Vriesea* species. The main attraction for gardeners is the glorious flower spikes which come in all the colours

Above: The deep purple of *Guzmania* 'Amaranth' contrasts well with the soft green leaves.

of the rainbow and last for months.

Many of the species are best suited for indoor conditions, except in truly subtropical or tropical gardens. While they may survive in temperate climates, the cold damage they can get on the leaves detracts from their appearance. A number of the hybrids, though, are tougher and can handle temperate climates, unless there are frosts or long periods of cold damp conditions in winter.

Guzmania 'Amaranth'

An older hybrid, grown in many millions by Dutch and Belgian nurseries over the past century, this is a stunning plant. It has deep green leaves which set off the dark purple flower bracts on a 50–60 cm stem; the flower bracts stay in colour for several months. As with many of the guzmania hybrids, it is very cold sensitive so should preferably be grown indoors or in subtropical and tropical gardens.

Guzmania bismarckii

Simply superb — there is no other way to describe this stunning plant. The arching green leaves are heavily patterned with ivory, and sometimes the plant looks more white than green. Given time and a favourable location, it can reach 2.5 m high, with a spread of up to 1.5 m. Unfortunately, as this is a true tropical, you will need to have this in a heated greenhouse with relatively high humidity unless you live in the tropics.

Guzmania 'Cherry'

An older hybrid that is still well worth growing for its stunning orange-red flower spike with broad heavily coloured bracts. In flower, a good plant of this hybrid can reach 60 cm high.

Guzmania 'Cherry Smash'

A stunning plant that has deep green leaves which set off the cherry-red flower bracts on a 50–60 cm

Below left: A breathtaking display of Guzmania 'Cherry' ready to be sent to florists throughout Europe.
Below: Guzmania 'Cherry Smash'.

for good reason. The glossy deep green leaves are attractive, but the pine cone-shaped flowerhead is a standout. The cone is predominantly fire-engine red, but tipped with golden yellow, with the bracts near the top having the most colour. The flower cone can last in colour for several months.

Guzmania 'Decora'

This plant has a soft-leaved upright rosette of green leaves, which become heavily flushed in wine red when grown in high light. The compact star-shaped flowerhead in rich red, rises about 10 cm above the foliage and contains clusters of yellow waxy-looking flowers. The colour lasts for many months.

Guzmania 'Fleur de Anjou'

One of the larger growing hybrids with rosettes of over 75 cm in diameter, it has reddish tinged leaves. The torch-shaped flower spike is quite large and very vivid in red, pink and yellow.

Guzmania 'Irene'

Glossy green leaves can form a rosette that exceeds 60 cm in diameter; and the flower spike is very striking with rose-pink bracts on a tall stem. As with most of these modern hybrids, this is very well suited to indoor growing, or in shady positions in a subtropical or tropical garden.

Guzmania lingulata

A variable small species that has been much used in producing many of the modern hybrids. The variety *minor* is probably the most commonly grown. The small rosettes of light green bear a low star-shaped flower spike of bright red with white petals, which stays in colour for months. Fast growth and dependable flowering make this a good variety for

stem. The flower bracts stay in colour for several months. As with many of the guzmania hybrids, it is very cold sensitive so should preferably be grown indoors or in subtropical and tropical gardens.

Guzmania 'Christine'

A beautiful Belgian-bred hybrid, with a small open dark green rosette. The reddish orange inflorescence remains in colour for many months. It is cold sensitive.

Guzmania 'Claret'

A lovely Dutch hybrid, bred for indoor use but will grow outdoors in warmer gardens. Green leaves flushed with reddish purple on the undersides and lower leaf areas in high light. It has a dense star-shaped inflorescence in claret red with yellow flowers.

Guzmania conifera

In the last few decades this has been one of the species sold more often by commercial nurseries, and

Above: This *Guzmania* 'Decora' hybrid exhibits the wonderful massed flowerhead of this group.

covering a palm trunk or tree fern wall, but it is also ideal as an indoor pot plant. A mass planting in a shallow bowl looks great. Quite frost sensitive but it can be grown successfully in some of the warmer temperate gardens.

The variegated form of G. *lingulata minor* is quite lovely also, as the cream stripes, and to a lesser extent the green, shade a deep pink when grown in higher light levels than usual.

Guzmania 'Luna'

A beautiful hybrid with deep green leaves. The flower spike has many bracts of deep red, almost purple.

Guzmania 'Mandarine'

A beautiful cultivar of G. *lingulata* var. *minor* with a small, open, light green rosette with reddish orange inflorescence, and the coloration extends down into the upper leaves.

Right: *Guzmania* 'Irene' is almost neon in appearance.
Below: The vibrant colour of *Guzmania* 'Mandarine'.

Guzmania 'Ostara'

Light green leaves form a medium-sized rosette on this guzmania, and a slight copper tinge develops if grown in medium to high light. The flower spike is similar to 'Orangeade' but is a slightly hotter orange and has longer and larger recurving bracts.

Guzmania 'Pax'

A Dutch hybrid introduced in 1994, this is a relatively tender plant, with tall flower spikes of green, fading up to lemon and finally a star of lovely cream bracts at the top.

Guzmania monostachia

This small plant has thin green leaves, out of which a torch-like flower spike appears. The stem bracts are green, striped with dark burgundy and from which white petals appear. As the flower stem grows, the topmost bracts become progressively redder, finishing with bright fire-engine red at the top. It has one of the more unusual and striking flowers of the *Guzmania* genus. Reasonably hardy, it can handle temperate climates, but not frost. Excellent as an epiphyte or pot plant, it has very prolific pupping. Look out for a lovely variegated form.

Guzmania 'Orangeade'

Another old but exceptionally good hybrid. It has pale green leaves which form a medium-sized rosette above which the magnificent orange-red flower spike simply glows. Bright yellow petals appear from within the bracts. I have seen flower spikes stay in colour for more than 12 months. A variegated form is sometimes available.

Top left: *Guzmania* 'Orangeade' is very showy and long lasting.
Above: *Guzmania* 'Ostara' has a striking shade of orange to the bracts.

Guzmania sanguinea

A fabulous guzmania that always draws attention and comment when in flower. Unlike most others in the genus, this species flowers in a similar fashion to neoregelias, ie in the centre of the plant. In addition, although the orange-yellow flowers are quite pretty, most of the glory of this plant arises from the leaves, which start out leathery and green, but develop the most vibrant shades of yellow, orange and red at flowering, with the greatest intensity of colour developing in the centre. The overall appearance often leads it to being mistaken for a neoregelia. Unfortunately, it is very slow to reproduce, usually having only one or two pups which develop near the centre of the plant. It also has the unfortunate habit of rotting in the centre at flowering, which can be avoided by keeping the centre dry once flowers are seen. Reasonably hardy, it can handle temperate climates but not frost. It is excellent as an epiphyte or pot plant.

There is a smaller form available, G. sanguinea var. brevipedicellata, which has bright red leaves and no shading to yellow.

Guzmania squarrosa

An impressive plant that can reach up to 1 m wide. The flower spike is thick and cylindrical, mostly green, with tinges of yellow except for the large stem bracts which are bright red. Quite hardy for this genus, it can handle light frosts, and is suitable for growing both in the ground and in trees.

Guzmania 'Ultra'

One of the best purple-flowered bromeliads. The fairly small rosettes of deep green leaves carry a short but very dense spike of deep purple bracts.

Guzmania wittmackii

A relatively large guzmania, with a tall flower spike and prominent lilac-purple bracts which remain in colour for months. The medium-sized rosette consists of glossy deep green leaves. There are many other colour forms of this species, including amethyst, orange, red, rose and yellow. This species has produced many hybrids, and fortunately is a little more cold resistant than some; it can be successfully grown in shady, warm temperate gardens.

Guzmania zahnii

This species has lovely foliage with fine lines of reddish brown overlaid on the soft green leaves. It also has the most gorgeous flower spike, with large red bracts and golden yellow flowerheads. The stem stays in colour for six weeks or more.

G. 'Omer Morobe' is a dramatic cultivar of G. zahnii with longitudinal stripes of pink, green and white. It is often called by its old name of G. zahnii 'Variegata'.

Below: The purple flower spike of Guzmania wittmackii.

HOHENBERGIA

A genus of more than 40 species, these large and impressive plants resemble *Aechmea*, with their large tank rosettes and similar foliage. They are native to parts of Brazil, Central America and the Caribbean. Excellent for landscaping as they are tough and sun hardy; however, in most cases they are quite frost tender, so will need a subtropical garden or very warm temperate garden.

Above: The chocolate and silver of *Hohenbergia correia-araujoi*.

Hohenbergia correia-araujoi

Discovered in 1979, this is an extraordinary plant with stiff leaves of copper brown heavily banded with silver. The flower spike has a pink stem, tipped with flower clusters of silver. It can be grown either in the soil or as an epiphyte, but in either case it is best placed higher than the surrounding area in order to take advantage of the spectacular leaves and to keep the drooping lower leaves from sprawling over the ground.

Hohenbergia rosea

A large species of bromeliad from Bahia, Brazil, which has a well-shaped rosette up to 1.2 m wide. The leaves are a rusty burgundy colour with slight mottling. The flower spike is quite stunning with deep red clusters of flowers scattered up the stem. An excellent plant for large, open gardens, it prefers light shade for best leaf colour.

Hohenbergia stellata

A beautiful plant from Venezuela and northern Brazil. It has reasonably ordinary olive-green leaves, but the stunning flower spike more than makes up for the drab foliage and makes this one of the most popular garden plants in the genus. The tall flower spike carries large tufts of scarlet-red bracts and purple flowers, which are so vibrant that they are visible from great distances.

xNEOMEA

xNeomea is an intergeneric cross between Neoregelia and Aechmea. The hybrids usually combine the vibrant leaf colours of the neoregelia parent, with the leaf shape and patterning of the aechmea parent. Many of these hybrids have been created from Aechmea recurvata and its cultivars, which make them quite hardy and able to take full sun. However, a few that have been hybridised with A. chantinii need to be treated more carefully. Most of these hybrids are still difficult to obtain, except xNeomea 'Strawberry'.

xNeomea 'Strawberry'

An intergeneric hybrid of Neoregelia carolinae crossed with Aechmea recurvata benrathii. Short, tough green leaves form a stocky rosette, which turns bright pink in high light. At flowering the centre of the plant turns bright red, with a slightly raised flower cluster of red bracts and purple flowers.

xNEOPHYTUM

xNeophytum is an intergeneric cross between Neoregelia and Orthophytum. Most of the neophytum crosses use Orthophytum navioides, which has rosettes of numerous narrow spiny leaves that turn brilliant red when the plant flowers. The offspring carry over much of these characteristics, but combine them with the ease of growth of the neoregelia parents.

xNeophytum are best grown in soil, which should be high in nutrients and humus. Although they can grow in full sun, slightly dappled shade gives the best-quality foliage.

xNeophytum 'Burgundy Hill'

Neoregelia 'Royal Burgundy' has been crossed with Orthophytum navioides to make a sumptuous plant. The spiky rosette consists of glossy, deep burgundy leaves up to 75 cm in diameter. It is still very hard to obtain, but well worth trying.

xNeophytum 'Firecracker'

Another Orthophytum navioides hybrid, this time crossed with the famous Neoregelia 'Fireball', so has the best of both parents. The narrow blood-red leaves are arranged in a pleasing rosette up to 30 cm wide, similar in shape but more open than the orthophytum parent. It needs full sun to get maximum colour. It spreads on short stolons, so is great for hanging baskets or planting in tree fern stumps.

xNeophytum 'Ralph Davis'

A superb hybrid with numerous stiff, narrow, dark red, almost purple leaves which form a rosette up to 60 cm wide. At flowering the plant blushes vivid red in the centre. Quite hardy but best in light shade, although it can take full sun if allowed to acclimatise slowly. It pups prolifically.

NEOREGELIA

All the *Neoregelia* species are tank-type epiphytes or terrestrials, with most native to south-eastern Brazil, and a small group native to the upper Amazon region. Most of this genus have relatively flat rosettes, but a number are vase shaped. This group of plants has the most diverse set of leaf colours and markings within the family, with spots, stripes and bands in all colours. At flowering, the central leaves of many species change colour, turning vivid shades of red, pink, purple and more. The flowers themselves are situated well within the vase of the plant and are therefore usually insignificant and inconspicuous, although quite pretty. Several of the species have a slight fragrance.

Although there are only about 100 species of neoregelia, these are among the most hybridised plants in the bromeliad family, giving rise to many thousands of hybrids. Many of these hybrids have only slight differences from each other, and with the tendency of neoregelias to change their appearance according to growing conditions, this makes identification and naming a very complex and often impossible task.

This page, top right: The deep reds of these two *Neoregelia* hybrids would make a stunning statement in any garden. Middle: This *Neoregelia carolinae* x 'Painted Lady' x 'Lilliputian' x 'Fireball' x *carolinae* x 'Vulcan' has a complex family history, which produces a striking result. Right: A small but very beautiful *Neoregelia* hybrid.

Opposite: A *Neoregelia marmorata* hybrid from Exotica, as yet unnamed, which has fine lines on the leaf in addition to the spots.

Neoregelia 'Amazing Grace'

Named after the Australian hybridiser, Grace Goode, this plant has a small- to medium-sized rosette with pale lime-green leaves heavily lined in deep red like a peppermint lolly. The whole plant blushes red in good light. In some sports of this hybrid, an entire side of the leaf can be one thick line of deep red. Reasonably hardy, these can be grown in dappled light or heavier shade without losing too much colour.

Neoregelia ampullacea

This small species is important for hybridisers who wish to take advantage of the stoloniferous growth form it exhibits. Discovered over a century ago, it is the parent of many beautiful little hybrids, many with very intricate markings. The species has very cute cylinders of green with dark horizontal bands. The banding is darker in full sun and the green portion of the leaves can take on a gold colour. It is exceptional for hanging baskets or in trees as it produces more cylinders from stolons which often hang lower than the parent plant. Some varieties are small, little more than a child's finger wide; others are broad, the width of a person's hand. Shape is very much determined by light also, with low light producing large but weakly coloured plants and full sun producing smaller but exceptionally well-coloured plants.

There are many varieties, including N. ampullacea 'Zebrina', which is one of the most striking. The dark maroon, almost black mottling and barring give an elegant rich appearance to the leaves as the background green nearly disappears.

Neoregelia 'Apricot Beauty'

This plant came to me as N. 'Apricot Beauty', but is most likely misnamed. However, the stunning dark, rich apricot leaves lightly covered in green spots are too good to leave out because of a naming error. When the plants are young, they may be more green than apricot, but as they age the colour develops and becomes most intense in full sun. A fairly tough plant that can handle light frosts and adverse conditions.

Neoregelia 'Avalon'

An older hybrid but still very worthwhile having in the garden. The wide leaves are deep, almost mahogany red all over, very lightly marked with lighter reds and greens creating a nice effect. Best in light shade for maximum leaf colour, it is an excellent plant for introducing intense colour to the garden.

Neoregelia 'Aztec'

An intense little plant that has been around for many years; however, many other neoregelia have been misnamed as this one, which causes confusion. It has a small rosette about 15–20 cm wide, dark red with many light green spots. A very hardy plant that can take full sun, moderate frosts, salt spray and just about anything else. It is excellent over rocks and as an epiphyte, but also makes quite an impressive border plant in more formal gardens.

Opposite, top: The glossy, vibrant foliage of *Neoregelia* 'Apricot Beauty'.
Bottom left: The dark bands of *Neoregelia ampullacea* show up much more when grown in full sun.
Bottom right: *Neoregelia* 'Aztec' is a vibrant and hardy hybrid.

Above: *Neoregelia* 'Beta' x 'Magnifica' provides sumptuous colour for semi-shaded areas.

Neoregelia 'Bea Hanson'

'Bea Hanson' is named after one of the first New Zealand bromeliad collectors. Young plants start off as green leaves, banded with very wide bands of deep burgundy, overlaid with spots and blotches of green. As the plants mature, the green changes to mahogany, and eventually the whole plant turns the colour of polished mahogany. It is striking at any age and good for sunny positions.

Neoregelia 'Beta' x 'Magnifica'

A lovely hybrid with very glossy leaves of deep maroon, shading to dark red in the centre, which turns scarlet red when flowering. Prefers dappled light to bring out the best leaf colour and to avoid sun scorch, but will still colour up reasonably well in dense shade. It can take light frosts.

Neoregelia 'Black Forest'

This hybrid has upright rosettes which grow to about 45 cm in diameter. The dark burgundy leaves have many almost symmetrical green spots. One of the hybrids from noted German hybridist, Dr Oeser, it is very hardy and able to be grown in full sun.

Neoregelia 'Black Knight'

Another older hybrid that is still very popular for garden use due to its very dark mahogany-red coloration and lighter red tips. It forms a flat rosette about 45 cm across and has faint spots of green; in some situations, the centre of the plant can be quite green, forming a nice two-tone effect.

Neoregelia 'Bobby Dazzler'

An outstanding Australian hybrid with a large, well-rounded rosette up to 75 cm wide. The leaves are heavily coloured in shades of blood red and mahogany, with small green spots and red leaf tips. Near the centre the green spotting coalesces into larger spots. Brilliant for full sun locations, where the intense colour will override anything else in the garden.

Neoregelia burle-marxii

For a more subtle effect try this species, named after the famous Brazilian landscaper Roberto Burle Marx. Only recently brought into cultivation, they are becoming more readily available. The rosettes are up to 40 cm wide, with green leaves lightly spotted with purple. In brighter light, the leaves take on a copper shade. At flowering the centre leaves take on a lavender hue, flecked with tiny spots of white.

Neoregelia 'Burnsie's Spiral'

One of the more unusual bromeliads, this small Australian cultivar of N. *carolinae tricolor* grows in a spiral pattern, never flowering naturally but continuing to grow upward, producing layer upon layer of thin tri-coloured leaves. Over time the lower leaves die off, with the plant eventually forming a tall stalk. Due to its slow propagation rate, this can be left in a pot for many years, attracting comment from all who see it. It is not as cold hardy as N. *carolinae tricolor*, and grows best in dappled light.

Neoregelia carcharodon

A lovely, large but quite variable species, with glossy rosettes of stiff leaves. The best forms are those with prominent spines on the leaf edges and soft bronze or copper colouring. It is reasonably cold hardy, and best planted in very light shade to bring out the leaf colour.

Top: *Neoregelia burle-marxii* has subtle markings.
Above: A top view of *Neoregelia* 'Burnsie's Spiral', showing the lovely spiral effect.

Neoregelia carolinae

Originally from the rainforests of eastern Brazil and probably the most well-known neoregelia, these plants have been in cultivation for such a long time that the original species has been buried by the hundreds of cultivars and hybrids that have been produced by nurseries around the world. Without exception, all the plants from this species provide a long-lasting splash of vivid colour for shady or partially shaded spots. The attractive shiny green leaves develop colour tinges in strong light, with the colour relating to the final centre colour. Depending on the variety, at flowering, the centre turns brilliant red, cerise, pink or lavender.

In the cultivar N. carolinae 'Marechalii', the leaves are often tinged orange red even before flowering. These are usually seed-raised plants and the centre of the rosette at flowering can display a great diversity of colours from rosy red to vermilion or reddish purple, fading towards the tips.

The variety N. carolinae 'Princeps' has long been cultivated and with good reason, as at flowering,

Top left: A fairly common commercial cultivar of *Neoregelia carolinae*, which is much used in the garden. Top right: One of the most sumptuous bromeliads, *Neoregelia carolinae* 'Princeps'. Above: *Neoregelia carolinae* hybrid planted among subtropical groundcovers.

the centre turns an intense amethyst.

N. carolinae 'Meyendorffii' is a long-established cultivar with relatively small rosettes of wide, glossy deep green leaves and typically a crimson-red centre at flowering. In high light the leaves will tinge strongly with the same colouring as the centre. The improved version *N. carolinae* 'Meyendorffii' (Spineless) is, as the name suggests, a spineless clone of *N. carolinae*. The variegated version *N. carolinae* 'Meyendorffii' (Albomarginated) has thick stripes of white down the side of each leaf.

N. carolinae tricolor is one of the oldest *N. carolinae*

Above: *Neoregelia carolinae* 'Tricolor' grown in nearly full sun.
Top right: *Neoregelia carolinae* 'Meyendorffii' (Albomarginated) shows its strong colours.
Right: The glorious colouring of *Neoregelia carolinae tricolor* makes it still one of the most widely grown bromeliads.

varieties, but still one of the most popular. It has stripes of cream and green overlaid with pink in good light. At flowering, the whole plant becomes tinged with red, particularly near the centre. In the form 'Orange Crush' the normal tricolor foliage has a reddish orange tinge, more pronounced in high light. The leaves are longer and more wavy than in the original 'Tricolor'.

Another form of *N. carolinae* which shows variegation is the 'Striata' group. These comprise a number of cultivars which exhibit varying degrees of red striping, from fine, pencil-thin lines to thick bands which cover most of the leaf. The colour of the striping can range from dark pink, through red, to deep burgundy and almost purple.

Neoregelia carolinae x 'Painted Lady'
A medium-sized rosette of deep red leaves, lightly flecked with green and a magenta centre at flowering time. A very nice hybrid that prefers medium light.

Neoregelia carolinae x 'Vulcan'

A lovely little hybrid with bronze leaves splashed and tinged with green, and a stiff-leaved rosette that normally doesn't exceed 15 cm. At flowering the centre turns soft pink, making an interesting contrast to the leaves. This is a good plant for small spaces, such as between rocks. Avoid full sun, but try to keep these in high light, as the bronze colour soon fades to green in the shade.

Neoregelia chlorosticta

Relatively small but colourful rosettes of red leaves peppered with green make this a colourful and interesting species. Closely spaced clumps are ideal for planting in trees or on rocks. There are many hybrids from this species, most of them quite excellent.

The cultivar N. chlorosticta 'Marble Throat' is an interesting plant with light green leaves, unusual for their heavily marbled centres of white and cream. Best colour is produced in full sun, but acclimatise the plants slowly.

Neoregelia concentrica

A favourite of landscapers the world over, these plants have large, tough rosettes of leathery leaves heavily blotched with dark purple to black markings, typically, but not always, in concentric patterns. The markings intensify in high light and at flowering, when the centre turns rich purple. In areas where the summer sun is not too intense, they can be left in full sun all day; however, in high light intensity climates such as New Zealand and Australia, the leaves may scorch in full sun. They are also able to be grown in shade, as the centre colour still develops well there, but the leaf markings which are so popular with this species will be less obvious.

There are very many varieties and cultivars available, with differences in centre colour and in rosette shape. There are also many hundreds of hybrids made with this species as one of the parents. N. concentrica 'Blue' is a very large variety with only a few, very broad leathery leaves that turn blue in the centre at flowering. After flowering is complete, the blue area slowly changes to ivory, which is equally striking.

N. concentrica 'Lavender Lady' is a beautiful cultivar, with apple-green leaves forming a compact rosette, which at flowering turns deep lavender in the centre.

N. concentrica 'Plutonis' is very widespread and

Above: A purple-centred *Neoregelia concentrica* hybrid is quite effective in a shady garden.

Opposite, top right: A beautiful, but as yet unnamed *Neoregelia carolinae* 'Striata' cultivar from Exotica.
Bottom: A new *Neoregelia carolinae* hybrid called *Neoregelia* 'Exotica Velvet'.

has a centre of deep purple and prominent dark spines. There is a red form of this variety also.

N. concentrica 'Dusky Form' has large, tough rosettes of leathery olive-green leaves heavily blotched with dark purple to black markings. The purple markings intensify in high light and at flowering, when the centre turns rich purple. One of the favoured landscape varieties as it is so tough.

N. concentrica x 'Marcon' is an excellent hybrid with broad green leaves, overlaid with copper and burgundy shades, particularly in high light. Tough plants that can withstand the elements.

N. concentrica 'Takemura' is a large cultivar with wide, bronze-coloured leaves, strongly marked and banded with black, which form a nicely shaped, full rosette. At flowering the centre flushes vivid purple.

Neoregelia 'Crimson Nest'

This plant has tapered crimson-red leaves tinged green that form a well-shaped rosette. The inner leaves turn dark red at flowering, holding the colour for many months. It does well in medium to bright light, but avoid midday sun.

Top: Several forms of *Neoregelia concentrica* 'Plutonis'.
Above: *Neoregelia concentrica* 'Dusky Form' is a tough plant with very heavily marked leaves.
Left: The very vibrant *Neoregelia* 'Crimson Nest' is best grown in almost full sun.

Neoregelia cruenta

This is a very tough plant, ideal for growing in full sun over rocks or similar. The leathery yellow-green leaves with dark red fingernails to the tips take on their best colour in full sun.

The red form, *N. cruenta* 'Rubra' is a stunning plant. The upper surface of the leathery leaves is a dark speckled red, while the underside is barred with silver. A tough plant which is excellent for harsh locations as it is native to the exposed sandy coasts of Brazil.

Neoregelia 'Debbie'

A recent hybrid, this is a stunning red plant with wide, glossy, dark green leaves which show tinges of red from a young age. At flowering, almost the whole plant turns vibrant, fire-engine red, staying that way for months on end. Ideal for bright shade in the garden, or as a pot plant indoors. Extensively used for interior landscaping in the United States; however, it is also capable of withstanding light frosts.

Neoregelia 'Dexter's Pride'

A very nice medium-sized rosette with leaves of an exceptional rich dark red, almost burgundy colour when grown in good light.

Neoregelia 'Dr Oeser'

There are many forms of this small hybrid in cultivation as it has been distributed worldwide, mainly by seed, which is quite variable. The foliage colours best in very light shade, just enough to prevent burning. These plants are quite hardy and able to take light frosts, and are excellent for pots or in tight spaces in the garden.

Above: *Neoregelia* 'Debbie' starts to show colour.

Neoregelia 'Fireball'

This small blood-red neoregelia is one of the most well known, and has been used in many hybrids since its discovery in the 1960s. The rosette stays green in low light and needs full sun for maximum colour. The pups develop on stolons up to the width of the parent plant, making them ideal for hanging baskets or growing on stumps and tree ferns. They also look fantastic scrambling over light-coloured rocks, where the growth habit and intensity of colour make them a real talking point. However, insufficient light and overfeeding can quickly make these plants turn green.

Neoregelia 'Fireball' x 'Avalon'

A good 'Fireball' hybrid with highly coloured reddish leaves splashed with green. Compact rosettes spread via stolons, making this plant ideal for hanging baskets or sprawling over rocks. It is quite hardy and adaptable to full sunlight.

Neoregelia 'Fireball' x 'Plutonis'

An unusually coloured hybrid with dark maroon, almost purple leaves forming a medium-sized flat rosette. Best colour is produced in full light, its very variable appearance depending on growing conditions.

Neoregelia 'First Prize'

A top-class red hybrid that starts off with wide, bronzy red leaves, speckled with bright green. As flowering approaches, the centre leaves gradually darken to a rich red, which evenly blends out to the bronze tips and lower leaves. Very good as a feature plant in the garden, but best in very light shade; tends to lose too much colour if planted in heavier shade.

Neoregelia 'Fosperior Perfection'

This is a sumptuous cultivar of 'Fosperior', more correctly just named 'Perfection', with richly coloured glossy leaves of deepest red, striped with scarlet down the centre of each one. Bright filtered light is best to keep the colour in this hybrid, which is still quite difficult to obtain but worth waiting for.

Neoregelia 'German Hybrid'

An unnamed but very nice hybrid that has been around for many years in a number of countries.

Many thin, glossy, solid red leaves form a nice rosette that is capable of keeping its colour even in full sun, which is unusual for the glossy red neoregelia cultivars, most of which prefer very light shade to do their best.

Neoregelia 'Gold Fever'

A lovely bright crimson Australian neoregelia hybrid with a multitude of lime-green spots. It has a compact, symmetrical rosette that grows to about 30 cm in diameter. When grown in full sun, the crimson turns deep blood red and the lime green goes almost gold. Very hardy and will grow almost anywhere.

Neoregelia 'Grace'

Another gorgeous recent addition to the *Neoregelia* genus, this has red-tinted, glossy green leaves when young, with most of the plant changing to hot, almost neon-pink leaves at flowering. Ideal for bright shade in the garden, or as a pot plant indoors.

Neoregelia 'Guinea'

This old, but very useful hybrid deserves a place in any bromeliad garden. It has small rosettes of light green, heavily spotted and tipped with fingernails of maroon. In full sun the light green foliage turns a glorious gold, making the spots stand out even more. Tough plants that can be grown in full sun, forming tightly knit clusters, make it brilliant for planting in trees or in gaps between rocks.

This page, top: *Neoregelia* 'Fireball' x 'Plutonis' has rich colouring.

Opposite, top: The neon colouring becomes more intense when *Neoregelia* 'Grace' flowers. Bottom left: *Neoregelia* 'Guinea' develops dramatic gold and rusty colours if grown in full sun. Bottom right: One of the most sought-after bromeliads, *Neoregelia* 'Fosperior Perfection'.

Neoregelia 'Hearts Blood'

A delicate and pretty miniature hybrid. The name is appropriate, as at flowering, the centre of the plant turns bright red, with speckles of blood red on the surrounding foliage. This small neoregelia is particularly well suited for hanging baskets, rock walls, placing in trees or on tree fern stumps. As a ground plant, it will eventually form a light attractive groundcover, particularly when grown on banks.

Neoregelia 'Hojo Rojo'

This plant has glossy, deep burgundy leaves which look awesome in the rain. It forms a small flat rosette, which spreads by short stolons, producing a

Above: The huge rosettes of *Neoregelia johannis* can reach nearly 1 m across.

carpet of burgundy rosettes over time. Flowers are violet, but generally insignificant.

Neoregelia johannis

Broad yellowish green leaves with rose-coloured fingernails and red spotting and tinting as flowering approaches. An imposing plant and excellent for full sun gardens.

Another *N. johannis* clone commonly grown in New Zealand has large upright rosettes of copper-toned leaves, overlaid with hues of rose pink, which create an almost red appearance to the plant.

Neoregelia 'Julian Nally'

Another tough neoregelia, this is a cross between *N. spectabilis* and *N. marmorata*. It has marbled maroon and green leaves with pink-red tips but not such obvious silver banding on the undersides as *N. spectabilis*. The flowers are violet, but generally insignificant. Ideal for rocky areas or steep banks.

Neoregelia 'Lamberts Pride'

Relatively small but highly coloured rosettes of glossy, copper-red leaves, are heavily marked with splotches and semi-bands of cream or green, depending on the light level. Under nutrient stress, the red may turn fire-engine red, which can look fantastic, but care is needed not to stress the plant too much. It is best grown in very light shade.

Right: *Neoregelia* 'Julian Nally' shows its soft marbling best when the sunlight shines through the leaves.
Below: The small rosettes of *Neoregelia* 'Lamberts Pride'.

Neoregelia 'Lila'

A hybrid with quite stumpy leaves, an upright form and upturned edges when they are young. As the leaves mature, they flatten out and develop an incredible glow of almost iridescent lilac pink near flowering. These plants prefer shaded conditions, with some morning or late-afternoon sun to maximise leaf colour.

Neoregelia 'Maggies Pride'

A striking bromeliad, with dark green leaves that have broad stripes of cream surrounded by more slender cream stripes, all of the cream being overlaid by pink. The whole plant tinges pink in good light, with the centre turning dark pink at flowering. Best grown in partial shade as full sun will cause burning. Ideal for slightly stressful situations such as growing among rocks or on tree ferns, as the pink develops much earlier than when grown lush.

Neoregelia marmorata

This is a popular plant that has spawned many hundreds of cultivars and hybrids. It has heavily marbled foliage, dark maroon overlaid with so many green spots as to give the effect of green leaves marbled with maroon. High light levels increase the colouring till the maroon turns wine-red and almost glows. Stunning as clumps grown in full sun over volcanic boulders, but also quite effective as an epiphyte, as this is one of the many neoregelias that look great with the sun shining through their foliage. Quite hardy and able to take light frosts. Many of the hybrids and cultivars are very similar, varying only in the degree of spotting and marbling, causing many to be misnamed and renamed over the years. All of them, however, are well worth growing for those harsh spots in the garden.

Neoregelia 'Midnight'

A top-quality hybrid, with deep wine-red, almost black leaves when grown in good light. The leaves have a slight frosting of silver over them, which reduces their gloss, but makes them more resistant to cold and sun than would otherwise be expected with a plant of this colour. A good plant for using near lime-green foliage, as it makes a pleasing contrast.

Top left: A potted display of neon-coloured *Neoregelia* 'Lila' is stunning indoors or out.
Middle: *Neoregelia* 'Maggies Pride' has intense colours.

Neoregelia 'Mottles'

Stout, leathery, heavily spined and mottled leaves of dark maroon with green spots give this plant a striking appearance. The pups arise on short stolons, which make them very suitable for growing over rocks or as epiphytes. They have a hardy nature suitable for the toughest of landscapes; in fact, the harsher the environment, the brighter the maroon and the more golden green the speckling.

Neoregelia 'Noble Descent'

This long-established excellent hybrid provides a good contrast to most other neoregelia. Light green leaves, which turn golden yellow in strong light, provide an unusual background for light speckles of red, red leaf tips and a red centre at flowering. They are very tough plants which can be planted in full sun, or light shade; and will handle moderate frosts, salt spray and dry conditions with ease. Excellent for landscaping on rocky banks and in similar harsh environments.

Neoregelia 'Oh No'

Glossy, shocking pink leaves form a medium rosette approximately 30 cm across. The rounded leaf tips are slightly lighter in colour and the leaves have slight ridges down them. Suitable for semi-shade areas in the garden, these make a statement wherever they are planted.

Top right: *Neoregelia* 'Mottles' needs full sun to achieve maximum colour.
Right: *Neoregelia* 'Noble Descent' is best grown hard for maximum colour.

Above: *Neoregelia* 'Painted Lady' has a multitude of colours on each leaf.

Neoregelia olens 'Vulcan'

This very old miniature cultivar of *N. olens* has been recently renamed *N. olens* 'Marie'. The small, stiff, lime-green leaves turn golden yellow in full sun with red speckles and red tips. At flowering the centre turns crimson red. The pups arise on short stolons which make this little hardy plant ideal for hanging baskets, epiphyte planting or over rocks.

Neoregelia 'Painted Lady'

A fascinating hybrid with the most complex colour scheme of shocking pink, fire-engine red, lime green and grass green all on the same leaves. It needs to be planted where it can be seen close up to appreciate its intricate beauty. The glossy leaves are reasonably hardy, but best planted in very light dappled shade to bring out the best colours.

Neoregelia pascoaliana

A large neoregelia, which can achieve a spread of 60 cm or more, with wide, fleshy leaves which have a very unusual colouring of yellowish green with a pink tinge in high light. The leaves are lightly banded and speckled with fine reddish purple spots and reddish leaf tips. Reasonably hardy and able to take full sun. Best as a feature plant due to its size and ideal as a large potted bromeliad. It is slow to pup.

Neoregelia 'Pemiento'

A beautiful hybrid from the stable of noted American hybridist, Chester Skotak, which uses *N.* 'Royal Burgundy' extensively in its pedigree. The glossy leaves have rich deep burgundy edges and a broad central stripe of vivid red. Very beautiful, although it can be difficult to come by. Best in light shade to prevent burning.

This page, below: *Neoregelia olens* 'Vulcan' is a small plant, but has very intense colouring at flowering time.

Opposite, top: *Neoregelia pineliana*. Bottom: A line-up of *Neoregelia* 'Purple Star' on a fallen tree fern log.

Neoregelia pineliana

Although grown for many years under this name, in fact it is most probably *N. farinosa*. A wide rosette, up to 60 cm across, is comprised of numerous, quite slender, dusty green leaves. At flowering, the centre turns bright red. Quite hardy and capable of taking moderate frosts, salt spray and wind. Best in dappled light as full sun may cause some scorching; also able to be grown in heavy shade with little negative effect. The pups arise from long stolons which often develop higher than the mother plant, so if placed by a tree or wall, the pups will grad-ually climb up. Alternatively, create a lovely staggered effect by planting on a stump or in a hanging basket.

Neoregelia princeps

This species has a flat rosette that can reach 80 cm in diameter, consisting of dusty green leaves, heavily barred on the underside with silver stripes which look great when viewed from underneath. The centre turns a spectacular bright lavender purple at flowering. A perfect plant for epiphytic planting, where it produces its best colour; can also be grown in soil, but starve it slightly to bring out the colours.

Neoregelia 'Purple Star'

This hybrid has wide leaves with a lovely half twist to them when young, which eventually straightens out to a wavy leaf when older to form a well-shaped rosette about 40 cm across. The leathery leaves develop a soft maroon shade in high light, and at flowering the centre develops shades of light amethyst and dark purple. Prefers shaded conditions, with some morning or late-afternoon sun to maximise the leaf colour.

Neoregelia 'Royal Cordovan'

A very well-shaped rosette of wide, glossy copper leaves, shading to burgundy when grown in high light conditions; the leaf tips are tinted red. At flowering, the centre turns fire-engine red. Best colour is developed in high light, with just enough shade to prevent burning; however, the centre colour will still develop well in low light conditions, making this a good plant for indoors or out.

Neoregelia 'Sailors Warning'

Relatively small, open star-shaped rosette which grows to a span of 20–25 cm. The glossy leaves are bright red with large green spots and longitudinal splashes. Best in full sun, where the most red will develop on the leaves, almost covering the entire leaf surface. Quite hardy and able to withstand light frosts. Excellent as a well-behaved pot plant for the patio or in a sunny border situation in the garden.

Above: The scarlet of *Neoregelia* 'Scarlet Charlotte' is quite intense.

Neoregelia sarmentosa 'Yellow Bird'

A compact rosette of leathery light green leaves, lightly spotted and banded with dark reddish brown, mainly underneath and near the centre. In full sun, the leaves turn a pale gold. It is very tough, although somewhat frost tender.

Neoregelia 'Scarlet Charlotte'

A stunning hybrid with perfectly rounded rosettes of glossy light green leaves, with nearly the whole plant turning a gorgeous scarlet pink at flowering. It is ideal as an indoor pot plant, or for intense colour under light shade in the garden.

Neoregelia 'Sharlock'

An older, but very good hybrid with fairly large upright rosettes to 50 cm diameter, of rich deep burgundy leaves with green spots and slight bands. The leaf tips are rich red. A striking plant in any situation, but best suited to high light, preferably full sun.

Neoregelia 'Sharlock' x 'Painted Lady'

Rich dark red leaves lightly flecked with lime green near the centre and flecked with burgundy on the remainder of the leaves. At flowering the centre turns a purple shade of burgundy.

Right: *Neoregelia* 'Sharlock' has an excellent deep colour for creating impact.
Below: The dark burgundy of *Neoregelia* 'Sharlock' contrasts well with lighter greens in behind.

Neoregelia spectabilis

Another plant that has been grown for many years, this is a tough customer, often called the painted fingernail plant for its pink or red leaf tips. The underside of the leaf is maroon with white cross bands. Ideal for rocky areas, but also good as an epiphyte where the distinctive leaf patterning can be better seen. There is a variegated form which is quite lovely, the variegation being relatively subtle compared to other variegated neoregelia.

Left: *Neoregelia spectabilis* is ideal for planting in lightly shaded areas.
Below: *Neoregelia* 'Short & Sweet' will eventually cover this tree fern stump.

Neoregelia 'Short & Sweet'

A gorgeous miniature hybrid with glossy green leaves that turn the colour of a good red wine in full sunlight. The mother plant sends its pups out on long stolons, which are quite capable of growing without a root system of their own. It is particularly well suited for hanging baskets, rock walls, placing in trees or on ponga stumps. As a ground plant, it will eventually form a light groundcover, which looks very attractive, particularly on banks.

Neoregelia 'Stoplight'

This plant is quite literally like a stoplight with its glossy green leaves with scarlet tips, forming a medium to large rosette. The centre turns bright pink at flowering.

Neoregelia 'Stormy Weather'

A small neoregelia with tough olive-green leaves, heavily coloured with purple-brown spots. In full sun and situations of nutrient stress, the leaves will develop a reddish cast over the other colours, making quite a complex colour scheme. Quite tough and suitable for sunny exposed sites that may be dry, windy or exposed to frost.

Neoregelia 'Takemura Grande'

An old but very good hybrid that has stood the test of time. Thick, leathery wide leaves in an almost metallic-looking greyish bronze tone, which in high light goes dark purple, nearly black on the outer half of each leaf. It is a very tough and hardy plant which can take full sun.

Top right: *Neoregelia* 'Stormy Weather' is aptly named.
Right: The leathery leaves of *Neoregelia* 'Takemura Grande' make a tough statement.

Above: *Neoregelia* 'Tangerine'.

Neoregelia 'Tangerine'

From an early age, this hybrid starts showing its true colours, with soft tangerine blushing over the green leaves. At maturity, the whole plant is covered in sumptuous mottled shades of orange, peach, red and tangerine. Best in dappled light, ideal for indoors or slightly shaded gardens.

Neoregelia tigrina x 'Fireball'

A miniature hybrid which is quite similar to *N.* 'Hearts Blood', but the leaves are more rounded and the centre turns an amethyst colour at flowering, with speckles of dark red on the surrounding foliage.

Neoregelia 'Truly'

In full sun, these miniature neoregelia glow, with golden leaves spotted with dark blood-red spots, so heavy at the centre and the tips that it becomes solid colour. Very tough and ideal for epiphyte planting.

Neoregelia 'Ultima'

Very beautiful plants with thick cream stripes running down the centre of each leaf; in good light the cream becomes tinted with pink. At flowering, the centre turns cherry red. The pups arise off short stolons, so this is a good variety for scrambling over hard objects such as pots, stumps and rocks. Best in light shade, with maybe some direct sun in the morning.

NIDULARIUM

The genus *Nidularium* is one of the smaller in the Bromeliad family, with approximately 45 species. They are mostly epiphytes from the lower canopy of Brazilian rainforests.

Unfortunately this genus is often overlooked in the garden, which is a pity as it contains some very pretty plants, with flower spikes that last in colour for many months and attractive, well-shaped rosettes. There are several varieties with nice variegations and some with lovely deep burgundy colouration. All nidularium prefer shade and this is one of their best attributes, as these plants will thrive where many others succumb to a lack of light.

In addition to these qualities, almost without exception, nidularium can handle temperate climates. Some species have survived under trees where temperatures have briefly plummeted to -7°C. They can all cope with salt spray, some wind and a moderate amount of dry weather.

Nidularium amazonicum

Formerly named *Wittrockia amazonica*, the olive-green leaves with burgundy edges on top and rusty red colouring underneath make this an attractive plant. It is similar to *N. innocentii*, which has white flowers as opposed to the green flowers of this species. While an excellent plant and surprisingly hardy to cold given its soft leaves, it unfortunately tends to mark easily. Drought or any toxic compounds which fall into the vase will cause concentric brown patches to occur on the leaves later, when the damage grows out, so is best grown in reasonably humid situations to avoid this.

Nidularium antoineanum

This species has an upright vase of medium green, with lightly serrated and mottled foliage. A gorgeous star-shaped flower spike, held close to the vase, starts off pink before turning a most unusual shade of purple or mauve as it ages; the flower petals are clear blue. One of the more unusual bromeliad flower colours, so place it where it can be seen; looks brilliant under tree ferns or palms, or as a potted plant.

Nidularium fulgens

This is quite simply a stunner, one of the best of this genus. The leaves are grass green, beautifully spotted with forest green and with prominent but soft spines down the edges. Nestled in the distinctive foliage at flowering time is a star of fire-engine red, which lasts for more than six months, fading to cerise as it ages. A great plant for bordering shady pools or ferneries. Look out for a variety occasionally available with orange flowerheads.

Nidularium innocentii

This is quite a variable species, and the most common form has dark green leaves edged with reddish brown and rusty red undersides. Another common form has soft green leaves. The nestled flower bracts are usually deep or rusty red with white petals.

The variety *N. innocentii* var. *lineatum* has pale green leaves heavily lined with white — from a distance the whole plant appears to be creamy white. At flowering the tips of the central bracts turn rusty red. Quite a stunning plant, but more tender than the species.

Another variegated variety is *N. innocentii* var. *striatum* which is the largest of this species. The plants can reach up to 60 cm high and wide and have the unusual habit of forming a stem under the foliage over time; this stem can reach a height of 30 cm or more. The variegation is much coarser than in the previous variety, and cream rather than white.

The small cultivar *N. innocentii* 'Nana' makes up for its size by its beauty. The compact rosette is comprised of many glossy, deep burgundy leaves, topped with a star-shaped bright red flower with white petals. With its small size and need for high humidity, this is a very good cultivar for terrariums.

Left: The dark form of *Nidularium innocentii*.
Below: *Nidularium longiflorum* is closely related to *Nidularium innocentii*.

Nidularium 'Leprosa'

Attractive glossy green leaves lightly spotted with distinctive purple-brown spots form a large rosette up to 50 cm across. The peach flower spike sits well down in the plant and is also lightly spotted. However, the most stunning feature are the very unusual orange flower petals which appear out of the bracts over several weeks. Prefers a shady position, although a little direct sun in the early morning does develop the leaf spots better.

Nidularium 'Lila Rosea'

A gorgeous nidularium which is probably a cultivar of *N. meeanum*, with thin, fresh green leaves forming a tubular-shaped rosette. At flowering, long-lasting splashes of rose pink develop on the leaf-like bracts nearest the flowers. Great for shady areas or ideal as a pot plant indoors; also more epiphytic in nature than most other nidulariums, so suitable for planting on tree fern stumps or similar.

Top: *Nidularium* 'Lila Rosea'. Above: The unbelievable colour combination of *Nidularium* 'Leprosa'.

Top: The intense red star of *Nidularium* 'Madame Robert Morobe'.
Above: *Nidularium purpureum*.

Nidularium 'Madame Robert Morobe'

A large hybrid that can reach a span of 1 m when fully grown. Broad deep green leaves set off the star-shaped deep red flower spike, which sits just above the foliage. Reasonably hardy, although the leaves do mark easily. Great as an accent plant in shady places.

Nidularium procerum

Similar to *N. terminale* (which may actually be a hybrid of *N. procerum*), but the leaves tend to be thinner and longer, with slightly more colour. The flower bracts are also longer and thinner, making for a more open star of brick red, out of which appear lovely blue flowers. Copes with light frosts, salt spray and some direct sun.

   N. lubbersii is very similar to *N. procerum* and is probably just a form of it.

Nidularium purpureum

A small species with eye-catching metallic-purple leaves, very glossy underneath but with a velvet appearance on the top. At flowering the rosette is topped with a star-shaped brick-red flower with red petals. There is currently confusion over the naming of this species, which may in fact be a cultivar of another altogether.

Nidularium 'RaRu'

This plant has light green leaves with darker green mottling, and a star-shaped, dark rusty red flower spike with light pink petals. Similar in many respects to *N.* 'Something Special'.

Above: *Nidularium rutilans* is excellent as a groundcover.

Nidularium 'Rusty'

This plant with its serrated leaves that turn burgundy in high light is excellent for adding colour interest to a green area. Star-shaped brick-red flowers held above the foliage last in colour for many months. It is quite a tough nidularium that can be grown in some direct sun and is capable of coping with moderate frosts, salt spray and wind.

Nidularium rutilans

The glossy, star-shaped, bright red flower spike stands out well above the dark green mottled leaves. From the star comes white flowers with a slight pink tinge. This is a variable species with several forms, including the larger, more spotted version which was known as *N. regelioides* and the form with bright red petals, known as 'Sao Paulo'. The variegated form of this species is quite distinguished. All of them are lovely plants that are well suited to shady areas of the garden.

Nidularium 'Something Special'

This plant has a medium-sized rosette of shiny green leaves. It is similar to *N. rutilans*, but with more compact flower bracts which start out pale pink, gradually deepening in colour until it reaches deep red, finally turning burgundy. Quite a hardy hybrid, capable of taking light frosts.

Nidularium terminale

Scarlet, slightly dusty looking star-shaped red flowers which last for months, are held well above the attractive serrated light green leaves. It is a very hardy plant that can take moderate frosts and some direct sun, as well as dry conditions.

Top: *Nidularium terminale* is a tough plant for difficult areas. Above: *Nidularium* 'Something Special' with full bract colour, about to flower.

NIDUREGELIA OCHAGAVIA

There are a number of intergeneric crosses between *Nidularium* and *Neoregelia*, which are given the bigeneric name of *Niduregelia*. They are quite attractive plants and have the advantage of being more sun tolerant than *Nidularium*.

Niduregelia 'Sunrise'

An intergeneric cross between *Nidularium fulgens* and *Neoregelia spectabilis* produces this stunning plant. It has stiff, pointed rosy leaves that intensify in high light. At flowering, the centre leaves turn almost red. It can be grown in full sun.

Niduregelia 'Sunset'

This hybrid comes from the same cross as the one above, but has quite different characteristics. It has much wider leaves that are tinged pink with pink tips, and is less sun tolerant than 'Sunrise'.

A very small genus of only three species, originating from central and southern Chile, these are useful succulent-looking plants for sunny gardens, and look great mixed with cacti or other succulents. They come from harsh environments and can be grown successfully even in cold climates.

Ochagavia carnea

Stiff spiny leaves form a very tough plant that is reasonably frost resistant. The fist-sized flower spike is rosy red, with pink or mauve petals and bright yellow stamens.

Ochagavia elegans

Stiff spiny leaves with silver underneath make a solid rosette; the violet-pink flowerhead is nestled in the foliage. The plant creeps along the ground on a long stem, which is quite useful for growing over cliffs.

Below: *Ochagavia carnea*, covered in red flower spikes during late winter and spring, makes a solid border.

ORTHOPHYTUM

Native to Brazil, this is a small genus of less than 20 species of spiny but brittle-leaved plants that are great for covering rocky gardens and sunny areas, similar to their natural environment.

Although most of them are quite striking plants, which adapt easily to temperate and dry subtropical gardens, they are still relatively uncommon in cultivation, apart from the following two species.

Orthophytum gurkenii

A small but dramatic terrestrial bromeliad. The leaves are patterned with wavy bands in chocolate and white. At flowering, the plant becomes elongated with leaves appearing nearly the whole way up the stem. Great for growing in a rockery.

Orthophytum saxicola

The leaf edges of this species appear spiny, but in fact are quite soft, like *Nidularium fulgens*. It has gorgeous little stars of translucent orange. It is a very prolific plant; and some of the closely held pups form a ball of spiky foliage over time. This species also sends some of its pups out on long stolons, making it ideal to use over the edge of a wall. Also, as the name *saxicola* suggests, this little beauty will be quite happy scrambling over and around rocks; however, it still needs contact with the soil to draw its sustenance.

Top: The fertiliser prill (top right) gives some idea of how small these little *Orthophytum saxicola* are.
Below: Like chocolate-ripple ice cream, *Orthophytum gurkenii* is an unforgettable experience.

PITCAIRNIA

The *Pitcairnia* genus was one of the first to evolve and it is the second largest in the Bromeliad family with more than 320 species. This genus is a collection of oddballs though, as it contains many species that don't conform to our expectations of what a bromeliad should look or act like. There are pitcairnias that have leaves similar to other plants, ie with a leaf stalk and leaf blade; there are deciduous species; there are plants that prefer wet ground, as opposed to the rest of the family, and there is one pitcairnia that is native to west Africa. Some have spines, others have smooth leaves and yet others have both spines and smooth leaves. This genus confounds nearly every generalisation there is about bromeliads.

Pitcairnias are also one of the least hybridised and least grown bromeliads, the main reason being the grass-like foliage of most types and the short-lived flowers. However, when considering plants from this genus, compare them to other garden plants, such as ornamental grasses or flaxes rather than other bromeliads. They are certainly most capable of being added to any garden.

They are particularly well suited to wetter soils, as many of them are native to stream sides and wet areas. With their soft foliage and dramatic flowers, they are excellent near pools and in shady moist spots. All of them are terrestrials and need room for their extensive root systems, so life in a pot is not a good long-term option.

Pitcairnia atrorubens

A large-sized plant up to 1 m across and high, with unusual foliage for a bromeliad. The sprawling

Above: *Pitcairnia viridiflora* has an unusual green spear, with slender petals of lighter green that appear from each bract.

leaves start as thin stalks near the base, opening up to a lance shape. The flower stalk consists of a thick stem of closely packed red bracts shading to almost black at the tips, with small pale yellow flowers peering out from each bract.

Pitcairnia flammea

This native of eastern Brazil has tall, graceful, arching leaves of deep green, perfect as a background for the profuse, nearly 50 cm-high vivid-red flower spikes. This species loves moist soil and shady conditions, and is one of the most attractive members of this genus, very well suited to the garden.

Pitcairnia heterophylla

One of the more unusual bromeliads, native from southern Mexico to Panama, and Venezuela to northern Peru. It is known as *heterophylla* due to its habit of producing two types of leaves. One set of leaves is needle sharp and spiny and held close to the base of the plant. The other set is arching and grass-like, reaching up to 70 cm long. It is one of the few deciduous bromeliads, losing its leaves in late winter to late spring. Salmon-coloured flowers appear in clumps above the spines after leaf fall, and can be quite showy, with bright yellow stamens. Once the rainy season starts, the grass-like leaves appear. It is easy to grow and can it can adapt from full shade to full sun. Flowering is best in sunny positions, but the foliage looks ideal in shady spots.

Pitcairnia integrifolia

The grass-like foliage up to 60 cm high on this plant is fairly ordinary, but the tall spikes of vivid red flowers that appear in large numbers are anything but ordinary. Best grown in dappled light or full shade, but it can be adapted to full sun, where the green leaves will take on a reddish tinge. Best planted in moist soils with plenty of organic matter.

Pitcairnia tabuliformis

Yet another weird but lovely member of this genus. As the name suggests, the plant forms a very flat rosette, less than 10 cm high, with broad leaves overlapping each other with the effect of creating a living dinner plate. The green leaves are quite soft and tender, so this plant needs to be grown with care. At flowering, a lovely cluster of bright red or orange flowers, depending on the cultivar, arise from the centre, almost like a table arrangement. One of the side effects of the growth habit is that once mature, a potted *P. tabuliformis* effectively shuts out any water to the root system, so water must be applied from below to keep this moisture-loving plant happy.

Pitcairnia xanthocalyx

These plants eventually grow quite large, with grass-like leaves, moss green on the upper side and silver on the underside. Butter-yellow flowers are held on masses of tall flower spikes in mid-spring. They clump up very readily and like most pitcairnia love moist soil, so are ideal as a groundcover next to ponds or streams.

Left: *Pitcairnia flammea* is one of the more striking of this genus.

PORTEA

The *Portea* genus is small with only seven species, but it is spectacular. Porteas are all native to coastal Brazil where they grow on sand and rocks, usually in full sun.

They are almost all large plants, and combined with their toughness and appearance, they are very well suited to large-scale landscaping.

Portea petropolitana var. *extensa*

This spectacular plant, with large rosettes up to 1 m high and wide, is the most commonly grown of all the porteas. The flower spikes are spectacular, reaching 1.5 m and carrying many beautiful flowers; after flowering, masses of dark purple berries form.

Above: The colourful feathery flower spikes of *Portea petropolitana* var. *extensa* are an unforgettable sight.

PUYA

With over 160 species of *Puya*, this is a reasonable-sized genus, which provides some of the most fascinating and spectacular plants of the Bromeliad family. Among this group is the largest of the bromeliads, *Puya raimondii* at 3 m high without the flower spike and 10 m high when in flower, which may take up to 150 years to occur. Unfortunately, only a few are commonly grown, due to their large size and very prickly nature. However, with more interest in dry-style gardens, the smaller puyas will be seen more frequently.

Puya are, without exception, extremely hardy. They come from altitudes of more than 2000 m, where they are exposed to the harshest of environments, including desert conditions and snow.

Puya alpestris

From the Chilean Andes, this is one of the most bizarre bromeliads. Many times this plant is seen

photographed in small-town newspapers, when it flowers for the first time. A fairly large plant with spiky, silvery leaves up to 1 m high, it clumps vigorously from a young age and can quickly spread to several metres or more. Flowering typically occurs when young plants are 5–10 years old and one clump can have several flower stems. The flowers are what draw the attention, being the most unearthly shade of metallic-looking teal blue that has no equal in the plant world. The brilliant orange pollen liberally paints the heads of any birds that visit to sip the nectar.

This page, top left: *Puya* species form very effective groundcovers.
Above: Puyas combine well with *Furcraea roezlii*.

Opposite, top: The fat buds of *Puya glomerifera* about to come into flower.
Bottom: *Puya coerulea* in flower.

Puya coerulea

A large plant with leaves up to 1 m long; the leaves may be very spiny and turn a reddish colour in bright light. It produces tall, dark pink stems topped with violet flowers. This plant can handle very cold conditions without too much damage, and is an ideal subject for dry landscapes and rockeries.

Puya glomerifera

This fascinating plant has nicely shaped rosettes, up to 70 cm wide and high, of spiky green leaves with silver undersides, and forms dense clumps. At flowering, thick stems up to 4 m high bear fat light brown buds, out of which the large, dark metallic-blue petals appear. It deserves a place in any desert-style garden.

Quesnelia lateralis

The tubular rosette of green leaves, with attractive short black spines, has faint silver banding underneath which becomes more prominent in high light. Azure-blue flower petals contrast well with scarlet-pink flower bracts and stem on this winter-flowering quesnelia. A good landscape plant when not in flower and stunning in flower, it is a very tough plant and can cope with quite adverse conditions. It is excellent in rock gardens.

Quesnelia liboniana

This plant has slender tubes of green leaves, tapered near the tip. The curious flower spikes have only 5–10 flowers, but these appear as long tubes of reddish orange tipped with deep blue, almost purple petals. It looks quite interesting and is ideal as a pot plant or as a clump of epiphytes on tree ferns. It is very prolific, with the pups arising off tough stolons.

Quesnelia marmorata

This species is quite distinctive with tall tubes of black mottled and banded leaves, similar to a billbergia in shape, and its main feature is the lovely rolled tips to each leaf, making it look like a piece of abstract art. The pink and blue flower spike is short lived, but quite stunning. It is native to the coastal regions of eastern Brazil, and is therefore reasonably hardy. It grows very well in trees or over rocks, where it looks particularly curious, but is quite epiphytic, often not adapting well to growing in soil.

Top left: *Quesnelia lateralis* has the curious habit of flowering both from the side of the plant and from the centre, often at the same time.
Above: The striking form and foliage of *Quesnelia marmorata*.

TILLANDSIA

This is the largest genera in the Bromeliad family, and one of the most well known. The majority of the species are epiphytes, and mostly xerophytic epiphytes. These are characterised by their greyish silver-coloured foliage, due to the numerous fuzzy scales which cover the surface of the leaves. The leaves are often contorted into bizarre shapes. There is no tank for holding water and many produce little if any root system.

The other group are the tank-forming types, which usually have quite soft foliage in comparison to the xerophytic types. Most of these come from Central America.

Tillandsia aeranthos

These curious but lovely plants are commonly called carnations of the sky in their native countries, where they are quite widespread — in fact, they are probably the only bromeliad to have had a song written about them, fittingly a tango. The foliage is quite stiff, with grey-green leaves that keep developing in spirals, eventually forming long stems which curve according to light and gravity. The reason for their common name is the beautiful pink and blue flowers, appearing in late spring, which last a surprisingly long time. A hardy tillandsia which can take frosts and other adverse conditions, it is strictly epiphytic.

Top right: *Tillandsia kirchhoffiana* has slender green leaves which are more suited to shade than sun.
Right: This small clump of *Tillandsia aeranthos* is starting to form stems.

Tillandsia crocata

This lovely little plant achieves no more than 15 cm spread. The thin wavy leaves are heavily dusted with scales, giving a silver appearance; they tend to grow in one plane, giving the plants a flat appearance. It has single, saffron-yellow flowers up to 1 cm wide, which are highly and sweetly perfumed. *T. crocata* is easy to grow, being quite drought tolerant, and in its natural environment it is typically found growing in full sun over rocks.

Tillandsia cyanea

These plants are originally from Ecuador, where they scramble over rocks, and are now grown commercially in large numbers the world over. The small rosette of slender dark green leaves with maroon pinstripes clumps up quickly after flowering. It is one of the most striking tillandsias, with a spear-shaped lavender-pink flower spike and large purplish blue flowers. When these are open, the surrounding area is filled with a delicious scent of cloves; the flowering period can be more than two months. Can be grown either in pots, with free-draining mix, or as an epiphyte, and can be grown in a range of light levels, which makes them so suitable for pot plants indoors. However, low light and low humidity conditions result in pale pink flower spikes.

The cultivar *T. cyanea* 'Tricolor' has white-centred flowers. There are also white- and pink-flowered cultivars and many commercially produced cultivars, which may differ only slightly from each other.

Tillandsia deppeana

This soft green-leaved tillandsia grows to about 40 cm across and is often grown for the indoor pot plant trade. Its best feature are the lovely, heavily branched upright flower spikes with bright red bracts and violet-blue petals. It can keep its colour for several months after which it turns an attractive lime green. It prefers light shade.

Left: *Tillandsia cyanea* perched on the side of a tree fern trunk.

Tillandsia duratii

Strictly epiphytic, this stem-forming tillandsia grows up to 1 m long with tightly twisted leaves that curl at the tips. This habit helps the plant to cling to branches, as the dead leaves nearer the base curl around the branch. The stem ensures the tree doesn't outgrow the plants, so this sun-loving tillandsia is always present on the outer foliage of the tree. The erect flower spike bears many large lilac flowers. It is one of the most fragrant bromeliads, in fact a single plant can fill a small garden with perfume. This plant is also quite easy to grow and is very adaptable; it thrives under a wide range of light, water and temperature conditions, making it ideal for garden use.

In the variety *T. duratii* var. *saxatilis* the flower spikes are more gracefully curved.

Tillandsia fasciculata

A fairly large species with stiff grey leaves that may turn reddish in full sun. There are many cultivars and varieties of this widespread plant; the most common has a prominent branched flower spike of brick red and yellow. Prefers full sun but will grow satisfactorily in partial shade. Although very epiphytic, it can be grown in a free-draining medium.

Tillandsia filifolia

This small species has the finest of green leaves, almost the thickness of thread. Lavender flowers top a thin, branched flower spike. Can be grown in full sun or full shade, where the leaves can get quite long. It is best as an epiphyte, but will adapt easily to a porous potting mix.

Above: An unbranched cultivar of *Tillandsia fasciculata*.

Tillandsia flabellata

This variable species from the mountainous regions of Central America has both large and small forms, with either green or red leaves. It has multiple slim pencil-like flower spikes of bright red at flowering, out of which appear the small violet-blue flowers in late summer to autumn. It grows quite easily and can be used as either a potted plant indoors or as an epiphyte in the garden, but needs dappled shade and reasonably frequent watering.

Tillandsia foliosa

A lovely reddish green-leaved species from Veracruz, Mexico, where it grows at high altitudes of around 2600 m. The flower spike is crimson, with long, narrow, crimson bracts that curl down along the stem, out of which the bright purple flowers appear. It is somewhat similar in appearance to *Guzmania wittmackii* when flowering. It can be grown as a potted plant or as an epiphyte, but prefers high light levels to obtain maximum colour.

Tillandsia grandis

This is one of the largest bromeliads, and is another native of Veracruz, Mexico, where it is found on the rocky cliffs of steep canyons. The rosette of thick silvery green leaves can grow to over 2 m wide, but may take 20 or more years to do so. The flower stalk reaches more than 4 m high. Not too easy to get hold of, but certainly a spectacular feature in any garden.

Tillandsia imperialis

As the name suggests, this giant is an imperial plant, which comes from the cloud forests of the mountains of central and southern Mexico, and is usually found as an epiphyte, or clinging to rock faces. The light green leaves are tipped with red and at flowering are liberally and randomly splashed with more red. The impressive cylindrical flower spike reaches 50 cm in height and is fire-engine red; it can keep its colour for up to six months. Coming from such a high elevation, it actually needs reasonably cool conditions to thrive, so is best in temperate or cooler subtropical gardens. In their native country, these plants are often sold as living 'Christmas candles' for the Christmas festivities.

Tillandsia ionantha

This tiny tillandsia is one of the more spectacular. It has tightly clustered, small grey-green leaves that turn a flaming red at flowering; and will quickly form a tight ball of foliage in the right conditions. The colour is more intense in bright light. Relatively large violet flowers emerge from the top of the plant. It prefers full sun and must be grown as an epiphyte.

The cultivar *T. ionantha* 'Druid' is a lovely plant that blushes bright yellow when flowering, with pale yellow flowers.

Tillandsia ixioides

A small, silvery green, epiphytic tillandsia about 20 cm wide, which is widely found across South America, usually in dry woodlands where it can develop into huge clumps of plants up to 1 m in diameter. The leaves are quite brittle and stiff. It has small flower stems topped with bright yellow flowers. Quite adaptable to a range of light and moisture levels, but prefers full sun and the chance to dry out quickly after watering.

This page, top right: A fence post forms an excellent base for this clump of *Tillandsia ixioides*.
Right: A single plant of *Tillandsia ionantha* on driftwood.

Opposite, top: *Tillandsia flabellata* is one of the most appealing tillandsias, with its multiple flower spikes.
Bottom: It is easy to see why the stunning *Tillandsia imperialis* is used as a living Christmas candle.

Tillandsia juncea

There are many forms of this plant which are found from Florida south to Brazil. It has fine, grass-like, silver-grey foliage, which forms a feathery effect; the leaves tinge pink red in high light. The small flower spike sports relatively large amethyst-coloured petals. It clumps readily and is very hardy.

Tillandsia leiboldiana

A popular tillandsia that is sold in reasonably high numbers in Europe and the United States for its striking scarlet bracts and purple flowers. The flower stem can reach 70 cm high above the soft green leaves. In high light the leaves are blotched with red, although for best growth the plants should be kept in semi-shade. Although normally an epiphyte, it will also do well in pots or free-draining soil.

Tillandsia mallemontii

A small species, with silvery leaves that develop into a small ball over time, is from the Atlantic rainforests of Brazil. It resembles T. recurvata when not in flower, but is nearly always covered with many large mauve, fragrant flowers. A very easy plant to grow if good air circulation is provided. It prefers dappled light.

Tillandsia multicaulis

A particularly lovely tillandsia, native to the humid mist forests of southern Mexico to Panama, with soft green leaves forming small, well-shaped rosettes. One of its best features is its habit of flowering from the leaf axils as opposed to the centre of the plant. On a single rosette, several of the glossy, goldfish-shaped vibrant-red flower spikes will form, making a fine show. It is quite epiphytic, although it will adapt to pots in a very free-draining mix.

Tillandsia paleacea

These xerophytic plants come from the dry coastal deserts of Peru, Bolivia, Chile and Colombia, where they grow in thick drifts of millions of plants, receiving all their moisture from morning fog. The slender flower spike has fragrant lavender-coloured flowers. They are best grown as epiphytes.

Tillandsia punctulata

A tuft of thin, grass-like, arching green leaves, darker at the base, make for a graceful plant. The flower stem is brick red to about halfway up the spear-shaped inflorescence, then shades of deep green; dark purple flowers with bright yellow stamens appear at each bract. It is quite quick to pup, with the first pups appearing at the base before flowering. Prefers partial shade and reasonably cool growing conditions. It can be grown either as an epiphyte or in very free-draining potting mix.

Tillandsia recurvata

These tiny plants, widespread from southern United States to northern Argentina and Chile, quickly form tight clusters of stiff, silver-green leaves. The violet flowers appear on the end of thin, wiry stalks. It prefers full sun and must be grown as an epiphyte.

Tillandsia secunda

A large, stately tillandsia with stiff silver leaves that reaches up to 1 m across. Native to Ecuador, these large plants are often found perched on rocky cliffs and banks. At flowering the tall branched flower spike can reach 2 m high; after flowering has finished, numerous small pups develop on the flower stem, from the old flowers, in addition to the more usual pups which develop on the plant itself. All of the pups can be removed and grown on. Prefers full sun and is best grown as an epiphyte, although it is possible to adapt a plant to pot culture, with very coarse potting mix.

Tillandsia somnians

This curious plant has soft leaves of green, tinged with bronze in high light. At flowering, it sends its thin flower stalk as much as 3 m into the air and gets so tall that it needs something to rest against. The flowers are fairly boring, but pups develop every 50 cm or so along the flower stem, making this one of the few true climbers in the Bromeliad family. In their native environment, the plants simply sprawl over nearby shrubs, forming woven masses of stems and plants. Plant at the bottom of a palm or tree and watch as it climbs the trunk — quite fascinating.

Below: *Tillandsia somnians* clambers up trees with ease.

Opposite: The stunning *Tillandsia multicaulis* is best grown in shade, as it is here with these *Asplenium bulbiferum* ferns.

Top: *Tillandsia stricta* in flower.
Above: The fuzzball effect of *Tillandsia tectorum*.

Tillandsia streptocarpa

Native to the semi-arid regions of South America these are often found clustered on thorn bushes. The twisted clumps of leaves on this species always look slightly untidy, but this is remedied by the lovely violet-blue flowers with relatively large petals, held on a branched flower spike.

Tillandsia stricta

A hardy plant which has spread across most of the South American region. Perfectly shaped clusters of stiff, pointed, silver-green leaves form this small tillandsia. The flower bracts are bright cherry red, topped with dark blue petals; the flowers hang down from the plants, creating a nice cascading effect. Easy to grow as an epiphyte and very prolific; there are many forms available.

Tillandsia tectorum

This species has many different forms, and plants vary from as little as 5 cm in width to large plants of 30 cm. Fine tufts of thin silver-grey leaves create a fuzzball effect. The small flower spike sports a relatively large branched salmon-pink flowerhead, with violet-coloured petals. Clumps readily and is very hardy, its native habitat being the dry canyons of northern Peru and southern Ecuador, 1–2400 m above sea level. Here it grows in abundance and is collected by the thousands each year to simulate snow in nativity festivities. To maintain the lovely, snow-white fuzzy layer, the plants need to be grown hot, dry and in full sun, with minimal feeding; too much moisture, fertiliser and insufficient light will make the fuzzy layer disappear.

Tillandsia tenuifolia

This tiny species is widely distributed in woodland environments from the West Indies to Bolivia and Argentina. Clusters of stiff, pointed, silver-green leaves form huge clumps over time. The flower bracts are shocking pink, tipped with bright blue petals in early spring. This plant prefers dappled shade and frequent moisture and is best grown outdoors attached to trees.

Tillandsia usneoides

This is the fascinating Spanish moss that is seen in many films of the deep south of the United States. Hanging in dense strands from large oaks, these also do well outdoors in many other countries. The tiny plants are made up of silver-grey strands forming great beards of moss over time. Individual pieces can be broken off and hung over any object with ease. Over summer tiny yellow-green flowers may appear. When these appear in good numbers, on still days the musky fragrance is very appealing. Seed from this plant can be scattered over pine branches or similar and, with regular watering, will quickly form clumps and then strands. For best results, mist regularly with rainwater, or hang outdoors in the rain. Prefers light shade and good air movement. It does well when misted with a very dilute foliar feed occasionally. Wonderful for making living curtains to screen off unsightly areas or to create a mysterious entrance to a section of the garden.

Tillandsia utriculata

A large tillandsia which can reach a span of 60 cm. Clusters of stiff, pointed, grey-green leaves form open rosettes. The exceptionally tall flower spike, covered in yellow flowers can reach the height of an

adult man. Very slow growing and best grown as an epiphyte, it is usually grown from seed, as offsets rarely form.

Above: The giant form of *Tillandsia usneoides* has much larger leaves and stems than the more common type.

Tillandsia viridiflora

Soft, dusky green leaves with maroon undersides form an arching rosette, reaching up to 50 cm in diameter. The tall flower spike can reach up to 1 m; flowers are a beautiful shade of light green, with quite large petals. The mother plant sends up many grass pups before and after flowering, which can easily be grown on; several normal-sized pups also develop after flowering.

Below: *Tillandsia viridiflora* is best grown in shade; this one is about to flower.

Tillandsia xerographica

Native to the oak forests, dry woodlands and deserts of Central America, this silver-leaved plant likes full sun and warm conditions to bring out the pink tinges to the leaves. Endangered in its natural habitat, it is actually quite common in cultivation. The fantastic upright branched flower spike of gold with peach tones near the stem almost exceeds the size of the plant at flowering and lasts for several months. It copes well with plenty of rain over summer, but during winter prefers drier conditions. It needs bright light or full sun and good air movement. Slow growing, but excellent for hanging baskets or on tree branches.

VRIESEA

This genus is comprised mainly of tank-type epiphytes, some of which are huge. The leaves of the smaller types are often green, although some have shades of red or maroon, and usually come from the same habitats as guzmanias, in tropical rainforests. The larger species frequently have very heavily patterned foliage, often quite striking, making them very sought after. The flower spikes are usually sword shaped, sometimes branched, and the flamboyant flower bracts stay in colour for many months.

Although many vriesea come from shady habitats, most of them can actually withstand some direct sunlight. Some, mainly the larger, leathery-leaf types, can take full sun nearly all day. Their cold hardiness is quite variable and difficult to predict by just looking at the foliage — some of the seemingly more tender types are actually very hardy.

Vriesea 'Afterglow'

A striking hybrid from two very good parents. It has the colourful purple leaf tips and undersides of *platynema*, with dark green squiggles from the *fosteriana* parent on the upper surface of the leaves. The 1 m-tall flower spike has numerous deep red flower bracts with creamy yellow petals.

Above: A most attractive and unusual natural variation in *Vriesea hieroglyphica*; unfortunately, this may not carry through to the pups.

Vriesea 'Barbarosa'

This beautiful modern hybrid of *V. friburgensis* and *V.* 'Poelmanii' x 'Georgia' is a medium-sized plant which grows to about 30 cm across. It has slightly matt, dark green leaves tinted with autumn colours. The tall branched, deep red flower spike has yellowish shading to the underside of each bract and yellow flowers. It needs a warm garden to succeed and is best grown in shady areas.

This page, above: *Vriesea carinata* looks beautiful even before it reaches full colour.

Opposite, top: The deep red of *Vriesea ensiformis* with *Tillandsia cyanea* in the background. Middle: A beautiful hybrid of *Vriesea fenestralis* x 'Hawaiian Sunset'. Bottom: *Vriesea fenestralis* has intricate leaf markings that never fail to intrigue.

Vriesea carinata

A small but cute bromeliad, with soft light green leaves. The flower is a feathery fan-shaped spike, with red bracts at the base topped with bright yellow and green. It is very free flowering and holds its colour for six months or more over winter, so gives a lovely display in any garden. As the plants are so small, this is a good plant for tucking in little areas. Many hybrids have been produced using this plant as one of the parents. It originates from lower levels of rainforests of southern Brazil, at an altitude of 1300 m. This explains both its need for shade and its surprising cold hardiness, although frost will mark the foliage and temperatures below 2°C will generally kill them.

Vriesea 'Christiane'

One of the multitude of beautiful hybrids from Belgium that are grown in their millions. This relatively small plant has bright, glossy green leaves and a branched flower spike with paddle-shaped bright crimson branches. It is best grown as an indoor plant or for very warm and shady gardens.

Vriesea corcovadensis

A small vriesea with the appearance of a tillandsia, which reaches a size of about 15 cm across. It has stiff, pointed green leaves heavily speckled with red at the base, particularly in high light. The pale red flower spike is tipped with cream florets. It is quite hardy; and best in high light, up to full sun. The pups arise off long stolons, so the plant climbs well if placed at the base of tree ferns or similar. It is ideal as a hanging-basket subject, or as an epiphyte and over rocks.

Vriesea ensiformis

A lovely plant with a medium-sized rosette of soft green leaves. At flowering the sword-shaped deep red flower spike reaches up to 50 cm high; over time, striking tubular bright yellow flowers appear at each red bract. This species is quite tender, so is best grown as an indoor plant or for very warm subtropical gardens. Prefers shade and high humidity.

The variety V. ensiformis var. *bicolor* has orange-red bracts shading to yellow at the tips. It is slightly more tender than the species.

Vriesea espinosae

This epiphytic species is very similar to a tillandsia in appearance, and is native to the dry thorn forests of Ecuador and Peru where it grows in the thousands. It has stiff, pointed grey leaves, and grows to about 8 cm across. The flower spike is rusty red with several quite large blue flowers. The pups arise on stolons, forming lovely clusters reasonably quickly. It is best grown as an epiphyte, in full sun.

Vriesea fenestralis

These large plants from Brazil form rosettes up to 75 cm across. The curving soft green leaves are overlaid with many very fine lighter green stripes, with the patterning further complicated by numerous darker green squiggles across the leaf — very complex and pleasing to the eye. Under the leaves, light red spots complete the picture. As an indoor pot plant it always looks very glamorous; outdoors, it is best in dappled shade, with protection from frosts. Definitely a feature plant.

Vriesea fosteriana

These truly magnificent plants are native to the state of Espirito Santo in Brazil, and amazingly for a plant as dramatic as this, they were only discovered in 1940. Their native habitat is about 1000 m above sea level, which no doubt explains their relative toughness. Wide, sturdy mid-green leaves heavily banded in cream and reddish brown form a dramatic rosette up to 1 m in diameter. The flower stem can reach 1.5 m in height, with unusual cream flowers that open at night in order to be pollinated by bats in their native country. The bracts are usually cream spotted with purple spots. A quite tough plant that is hardy to -3°C if sheltered by overhanging foliage, it is best in high light or full sun for maximum colour.

Left: *Vriesea flammea* is strongly epiphytic and colours best when stressed. Below: The muted tones of *Vriesea fosteriana* blend well with just about any other plant.

Vriesea flammea

This small vriesea has stiff, thin, pointed green leaves with dark blood-red bases, shading to black at the bottom; the leaves are lightly speckled with blood-red spots. The flower spike is dark red-tipped with light cream-coloured flowers. The pups are produced prolifically on long stolons arranged symmetrically around the mother plant, resulting in a pleasing appearance to clumps of this plant. It is great for overhead planting or hanging baskets, and also excellent for covering rocky areas.

Numerous beautiful hybrids have been made from these plants, including the cultivar 'Red Chestnut', a superb plant with much redder banding than the species. The cultivar 'Vista' is very slow growing, with mainly white leaves with narrow bands of reddish brown. Another cultivar, 'Rubra', is one of the most well known of the *V. fosteriana* group, with its heavy chocolate banding.

Above: *Vriesea fosteriana* 'Red Chestnut' is a spectacular plant.
Below: This *Vriesea fosteriana* 'Rubra' is slightly stressed from growing in a pot in full sun, but this makes the foliage even redder.

Below: *Vriesea fosteriana* 'Vista' is slow growing, but well worth waiting for.

Vriesea 'Giant' x *platynema*

Despite its name, this is actually a rather small hybrid, with a rosette up to 40 cm wide of green leaves with maroon base and tips. In high light, the leaves take on a bronze cast. It has a reddish brown flower spike and bracts with yellow flowers. A fairly hardy vriesea that can take a range of light levels, light frosts and slightly dry conditions. It can be easily grown as an epiphyte.

Vriesea gigantea

A large and stunning plant that can grow to more than 1 m wide, it will always attract attention in the garden. The bluish green leaves are quite stiff and leathery, with an upright form. These plants can be grown in a range of light levels, but look their best when grown in dappled shade. They are quite hardy and capable of withstanding considerable wind, salt spray and dry conditions once established.

In the fascinating variety V. *gigantea* var. *seideliana* the rosettes of dark green leaves are marked with a network of white sections, which makes them look like they were originally white, then had green stripes and bands laid over them.

Vriesea glutinosa

Another gorgeous vriesea from the tropics of Trinidad and Venezuela, with thick brown banding on the undersides of the apple-green leaves. The rosette can grow up to 80 cm wide. The fantastic branched brick-red flower spike develops orange-red petals, with the whole spike staying in colour for many months. It is best in light dappled shade and protected from frosts. Quite epiphytic, but can also easily be grown in free-draining potting mix. Apart from the usual pups, this species also produces large numbers of grass pups, which can be removed and grown on like a seedling.

Vriesea 'Golden Pride'

A gorgeous hybrid with a branched flower spike in the most unusual shade of orange, shading to gold at the base of each bract. The soft green leaves are reasonably tender, so this plant is best grown indoors or in very warm and sheltered gardens.

Vriesea guttata

A lovely little plant comprised of light green leaves covered with small spots. The hanging lavender-pink flower spike is covered in a white powder, giving it a soft appearance; yellow-green petals emerge over time. It is ideal for hanging baskets or placed in trees so the flower can hang down.

Vriesea hieroglyphica

Quite deserving of its common name, king of the bromeliads, this is a dramatic plant with fascinating foliage. The rosette can reach a spread of 1.5 m, but will take about 10 years to do so. It has shiny green leaves, with dark, hieroglyphic-like cross bands. The flower spike is tall and branched, but is green with pale cream flowers, so uninspiring compared to the foliage. Ideal as a specimen plant in a subtropical garden or as a feature plant indoors. It prefers light shade, and copes with slight frosts if planted under overhanging foliage.

Top right: *Vriesea glutinosa* has striking leaf markings.
Middle: *Vriesea guttata* and *Tillandsia usneoides* are thriving in the coarse bark of a eucalypt tree.
Right: *Vriesea hieroglyphica* in the dappled light of a dragon tree.

Vriesea inflata

This species has a small rosette up to 25 cm wide, with soft light green leaves. The red flower spike shades to orange or yellow at the tips; it is semi-pendulous and has an inflated appearance, similar to a goldfish, which is the common name for this species. Frost tender and best in shade, so it is ideal for indoors or sheltered subtropical gardens. It is quite good as an epiphyte and with its pendulous flower is excellent for hanging baskets.

Vriesea 'Mariae'

A medium-sized vriesea with soft green leaves tinged with bronze in high light. The sword-shaped flower spike with a red centre and bright yellow tips lasts for many months. Prefers dappled shade with some morning or late afternoon sun. Looks stunning in bromeliad host trees.

Vriesea maxoniana

This pretty plant has light green leaves that form an attractive small rosette about 25 cm wide. The upright flower stem is distinctive for being a cheery bright yellow, fading to green as it ages. It is quite frost tender, and can be grown in soil or as an epiphyte with ease.

Vriesea 'Nova' x 'Red Chestnut'

This beautiful Hawaiian hybrid has the best of both parents — the leaves have the characteristic green with white sectioning from the *gigantea seideliana* 'Nova' parent, overlaid with a network of reddish spots, squiggles and tinting from the *fosteriana* 'Red Chestnut' parent. Quite hardy plants that need to be grown in high light to maintain the reddish tones. It is fantastic as a pot plant or in the garden as a feature plant.

Vriesea philippo-coburgii

A species with medium to large, well-formed rosettes of leathery leaves. In low light, the leaves remain deep green with brick-red leaf tips; in high light, the leaves turn light green, almost yellow, and the distinctive red tip becomes more prominent. Quite striking, particularly when in flower, as the red and yellow flower spike can reach up to 1.5 m high. It is quite hardy.

This page, left: Up close, the fine patterning of this *Vriesea* 'Nova' can be appreciated.

Opposite: *Vriesea philippo-coburgii* takes on a golden tinge when grown in direct sun.

Vriesea 'Plantation Pride'

This relatively small plant is one of the more successful recent hybrids, with its deep green leaves above which the large branched, bright yellow flower spike reigns. One of the most stunning yellow bromeliads. Sensitive to frost, and best grown in moderate shade, it is ideal as an indoor pot plant.

Right: *Vriesea* 'Plantation Pride' is a lovely shade of yellow.
Below: This red hybrid of *Vriesea platynema* is slow growing, but worth the wait.

Vriesea platynema

A gracious plant with large, deep green, almost blue leaves with faint banding, tipped with purple and with purple shading underneath. The 50 cm-tall flower spike has numerous purple to red flower bracts with creamy yellow petals.

The variety *Vriesea platynema* var. *variegata* is one of the more beautiful members of this stunning group.

Above: *Vriesea platynema* var. *variegata* is one of the most distinguished-looking plants for the modern garden.
Right: The delicate markings of a *Vriesea platynema* hybrid.

The variegated form 'White Line' is a superb plant, with thick white stripes down the centre of the leaves, making a stunning contrast to the red flower stem.

V. 'Barbara' is an outstanding wide-leaved compact clone, with a cluster of thick, deep red branches.

Vriesea 'Purple Cockatoo'

Light green leaves noticeably tinged with purple bronzing in high light, form a small- to medium-sized rosette. The flower is shaped like an upright cock's comb and is coloured purple.

There is also a 'Red Cockatoo' form, smaller than the purple form, which has light green leaves noticeably tinged with burgundy red near the base. The flower is also shaped like an upright cock's comb but is coloured bright red.

V. 'Pink Cockatoo' is less common, but also quite lovely with a nice pink colour.

Above: *Vriesea* 'Poelmanii' 'Selecta' in full glory.

Vriesea 'Poelmanii'

An old but very good hybrid that has been grown by the millions in Europe and the United States. It has a medium-sized rosette of light green leaves, slightly tinged with bronze in high light. The flower spike is spectacular, consisting of a tall, branched spear of glossy pure red from which poke bright yellow petals; the flower stays in colour for months. It is frost sensitive and prefers medium to low light.

The selected form 'Selecta' has more a compact flower stem, with the stem branches more horizontal than the original hybrid.

Below: The reddish tones and spotting of *Vriesea* 'Sanderiana' becomes more prominent in high light.

Vriesea 'Sanderiana'

This vriesea has light green leaves shaded purple, and lightly spotted with dark purple spots that can be seen on both sides of the leaf. The gorgeous deep purple flower spike is very long lasting, gradually showing yellow petals along its length. Unusually, the stem has a tendency to bend at right angles half way along, making it pendant. Relatively tender, so should be grown indoors or in a greenhouse in frosty areas. It is excellent in hanging baskets or as an epiphyte, where the hanging flower spikes can be enjoyed better.

Vriesea schwackeana x ensiformis

Gorgeous green rosettes up to 40 cm wide are topped with tall sword-shaped spikes of deep red. Yellow flowers complete the picture. A lovely hybrid that is best grown in warm shady gardens.

Above: *Vriesea schwackeana* x *ensiformis* just coming into full colour.
Left: *Vriesea simplex.*

Vriesea simplex

The apple-green foliage on this plant forms a small- to medium-sized rosette. It has a hanging flower spike, bright red with yellow petals which stays in colour for weeks. Ideal for hanging baskets or as an epiphyte.

The variety *V. simplex* 'Rubra' has soft leaves of olive green, heavily toned with burgundy.

a fire-engine red spike which is wonderful to behold. The leaves are darker overall than the previous cultivar.

Vriesea vagans

A small but pretty vriesea that spreads via long stolons. The bright green leaves have deep red, almost black bases. The feathery bright red flower spike reaches far above the plant and is tipped with yellow petals. Each mother plant will produce five or more pups at even intervals around the plant, giving an attractive appearance.

Left: A more slender hybrid of *Vriesea simplex*.
Below: *Vriesea* 'Favoriet' makes a bold statement against the cream wall.

Vriesea splendens

One of the more stunning bromeliads, with its heavily banded dark and light green leaves forming a medium-sized rosette, which produces a spectacular sword-shaped spike, typically red in colour. Particularly good as a pot plant or mounted on tree ferns or bromeliad host trees.

The fantastic cultivar V. 'Favoriet' has light green, almost cream leaves heavily banded with almost black green. A larger plant than the species, this has a rosette that can reach 60 cm in diameter, with an orange-red flower spike that can reach nearly 1 m high.

V. 'Splenriet' is also larger than the parent and has

Vriesea 'Van Ackeri'

A great hybrid produced in 1930, with a branched, burgundy-red, almost purple flower spike, out of which the bright yellow petals appear.

Below: *Vriesea vagans* shows the characteristic dark leaf bases and long stolons.

Vriesea zamorensis

A beautiful vriesea with clear green leaves tinged with red in high light. Magnificent in flower, with heavily branched red and yellow flower spikes that stay in colour for months. It is quite cold sensitive. Unfortunately it is very slow to propagate, as it generally only throws up one pup to replace the parent after each flowering.

WITTROCKIA

A small genus of only seven species, but nearly every one is worth a place in the garden. They are large plants with large glossy leaves, usually quite spiny and often very nicely marked. Most of these plants are adaptable from shade to near full sun.

Wittrockia gigantea

The large, full-shaped rosettes of wide, tough, leathery green leaves, are lightly spotted with blood-red markings, which are more concentrated near the tips. They are edged with blood-red, almost black spines. At flowering time the centre of the plant also turns blood red.

Below: Up close, the beautiful markings of Wittrockia 'Leopardinum' become more apparent.

Wittrockia 'Leopardinum'

This is a very exotic-looking plant, with wide, glossy, light green leaves, edged with black spines and dappled with large patches of dark green, almost black spots. The spots are more prominent near the tips, which are fully coloured. In high light the plant takes on shades of rose.

Wittrockia superba

The large rosettes, up to 1 m or more in diameter, of copper-coloured leaves, are mottled with darker markings and quite striking vivid red tips. They are edged with large red spines which add to their visual appeal, although admittedly less for their practical appeal. The flowers are held deep in the centre, with red bracts and white flowers. The best leaf colour is achieved in bright light, although avoid full sun as this may cause some scorching.

CULTIVATION

While bromeliads are generally easy care, there are some techniques that good growers use to produce top-quality plants.

LIGHT

The main thing to consider when choosing bromeliads for the garden is the amount of light, in particular direct sunlight, that the plants will grow in. Bromeliads come from a wide range of environments, from the deepest shade to the blazing sun of the desert, so there are species suitable for any light situation you may have.

Light intensity influences leaf colour, leaf shape and plant growth rates. Light levels that are too low for the variety will produce leaves which are long, thin and more green. Highly coloured varieties may lose nearly all of their leaf colour.

Bromeliads grown in light levels that are too high for the variety will produce shorter and thicker leaves. Excess light will bleach the natural leaf colour out of some varieties, particularly those with maroon on the underside of the leaf. Too much light may also produce yellowing or reddening on the leaves of some varieties as a stress response. Extremely high light levels may even cause leaf scorch, and this also occurs where a plant has been grown in low light levels and is shifted into high light levels without acclimatising it first, such as from a shadehouse into the open. In this situation, it may be better to delay planting out until autumn, when light intensity is on the wane, giving the plants six months or more to acclimatise before the next summer.

Plant response to light levels is also affected by temperature and humidity. In high temperatures and low humidity there is more likelihood of scorching and other plant damage from high light intensity. Therefore, it is much more likely that a plant will scorch on a dry, slightly cloudy summer day than during crystal-clear winter days.

Conversely, in low temperatures and high humidity, there is more chance of weak growth and disease in low light. This situation usually occurs in early spring and late

Top and middle: These two photos show an *Aechmea fasciata* grown in high light, with slightly reddish foliage and stiff upright growth, and one grown in dappled light, with a more open vase and greener leaves.

Above: Sun scorch first shows as a white patch on the leaves, which turns brown from the centre outwards.

autumn, and this is when gardeners are most likely to lose their bromeliads to diseases such as crown rot.

Nutrition also plays a very important role in a bromeliad's ability to withstand high light levels. Contrary to popular belief, most bromeliads will benefit greatly from good feeding. When well fed and grown in the most light that the variety can cope with, they will grow strong thick leaves with intense colouration. If underfed, green-leaved plants in strong light are more likely to turn pale green or yellow and are more likely to scorch. Coloured leaf varieties are also more likely to scorch if underfed.

Having said that, there are some special cases where placing particular plants under a high light, low-nutrient regime can be useful. For example, *Aechmea recurvata* and its hybrids produce fiery coloration under these circumstances, although they will also grow more slowly.

Similarly, many *Neoregelia* produce their best coloration in high light and low-nutrient situations, particularly those with either *N. marmorata*, *N. sarmentosa* or *N.* 'Fireball' in their parentage.

Some bromeliads have the ability to adapt to a wide range of light levels, and in these cases, the type of leaf that the bromeliad will produce will change from shade to sun. A good example of this are some of the *N. marmorata* group of hybrids. In full sun these have short, stocky rosettes with hard leathery leaves, heavily coloured with intense maroon marbling and spotting. However, if they are grown in shadier conditions, the leaves progressively get longer, thinner and less highly coloured. So where you chose to grow these plants is a matter of personal taste, as some people like the softer tones and contrasting colours produced by shade, while others prefer the hot vibrant colours produced by sunlight.

Another good example of this is *Vriesea hieroglyphica*. In strong light, the plants will have an upright form, with stiff straight leaves that are a golden green, overlaid with near black markings. In dense shade, the contrast is much more subtle, with light green leaves overlaid with dark green markings. While the first may sound more attractive, most gardeners prefer the latter, as the graceful, arching leaves of the shade-grown plant gives any garden an instant subtropical feel.

There are a huge number of plants in the Bromeliad family, each with their own 'best light level', and plant response to light depends on so many factors, such as nutrition, temperature and humidity. Also, the light intensity varies considerably according to altitude and latitude and even as the result of pollution from large cities. So how can the gardener work out what light intensity each bromeliad will like?

There is no substitute for experience and trial and error, by growing and shifting bromeliads into different parts of the garden. However, there are some characteristics of each bromeliad that allow the gardener to make some initial assumptions before choosing the right spot. The following table provides some categories for assessing the new plant, but remember that there will always be exceptions.

Leaf type	Plant location
Are the leaves mainly green, or with maroon or red underneath and quite glossy, soft and pliable?	Plant in full shade or early morning sun only.
Are the leaves highly coloured or variegated, but quite glossy, soft and pliable?	Plant where they can get morning or late-afternoon sun.
Are the leaves mainly green, but quite leathery and tough?	Plant where they can get morning or late-afternoon sun.
Are the leaves heavily coloured in red, maroon, yellow, purple or black and quite leathery?	Plant in nearly full sun.
Are the leaves mostly covered in white or grey fuzzy scales?	Plant in full sun.
Are the leaves very spiky and succulent in appearance, either green or coloured?	Plant in full sun.

Be aware, though, that when you first purchase a plant it may have been grown in the wrong light conditions by the original grower. This may result in a plant that looks green and soft, suitable for shade, when in fact it may just be poorly grown and will do much better in strong light.

Gardeners have the ability to alter light levels by planting in different areas, and planting or removing cover

plants above the bromeliads. This is one of the reasons why gardening with bromeliads becomes so fascinating and addictive — you are always wondering whether a little more colour, size or shape can be achieved by shifting the bromeliad to a new location. When design considerations, such as matching or contrasting leaf colour, flower colour and size come into play, it is little wonder that many bromeliad enthusiasts find that they shift their plants so often, it is better to leave them in pots!

Structures such as fences and houses can provide a solid block of shadow, which can be useful for planting, if the right plants are chosen taking sun direction into account. Therefore, sun-loving plants such as *Puya* and *Dyckia* species can be planted on the sunny side and shade lovers such as *Nidularium* and *Canistropsis* species on the side that gets no direct sun. Morning sun is great for those plants which need just a bit of direct sun to keep their colour, but not enough to burn, such as the softer-leaved *Neoregelia carolinae* types. Slightly more sun-loving plants such as *N. concentrica* and its hybrids can go on the side of the house which receives the late afternoon sun, thereby avoiding the burning midday sun, but getting enough direct sunlight to keep their intense colours.

Trees and shrubs also offer a wide range of light levels for the gardener. Heavy canopies are provided by large evergreen trees such as citrus, avocado, *Ficus* and many others. These are ideal for underplanting with shade-loving bromeliads, not to mention ideal for planting with epiphytic bromeliads.

Palms, tree ferns, cycads, cordylines and umbrella trees

Above left: A pair of *Vriesea fosteriana* 'Rubra' in the dappled light of a dragon tree and cycad. Above: A cluster of *Neoregelia* hybrids under the very light shade of a Queen palm get full sun for most of the day, except the midday sun.

provide a lovely dappled light which many bromeliads thrive under, taking up very little 'floor space' while providing both an ideal environment and great visual appeal.

Deciduous trees need more caution when underplanting with bromeliads. Some are very late to form their spring canopy of foliage. A good example of this is *Albizia julibrissin*, the silk tree. The new foliage may not provide shade till late spring, leaving any underplanted bromeliads exposed to quite high light levels at this sensitive time. Be careful also of subtropical trees such as *Erythrina* — coral trees, or *Annona squamosa* — custard apple trees, which lose their leaves for a brief time only, and in late spring, when the sun is strong and the bromeliads underneath may not be able to cope with the sudden increase in light.

Another potential problem with changing light levels is when a new garden is being planted. As most of the plants will be quite small, particularly those that will eventually form large trees, the initial shaded areas may be quite minimal. The natural response may be to plant full sun varieties. However, over time as the shade increases, these will lose their colour and become lanky and green. If shade lovers are planted, they will look scorched and stressed for the first couple of years. There are several options here.

Firstly, plant with a view to shifting as the light levels change. Alternatively, plant fast-growing species such as bananas to provide initial shade, then hack these out as the more permanent plants take over. Or, erect a temporary shade screen, using shadecloth over the plants, which can be done quite attractively with a bit of thought.

TEMPERATURE

Growing bromeliads outdoors, particularly in temperate or subtropical climates, can result in problems with cold damage. In general, bromeliads that come from either end of the bromeliad habitat range, ie those from the United States and those from southern South America, or from higher elevations on mountains in tropical regions are the most cold hardy. However, there are many exceptions to this rule, with some species from the tropical rainforests also proving to be very hardy outside their normal range.

The most obvious influence of the greenhouse effect on world climate over the past decade or so has been to increase temperatures overall. However, within that period many parts of the world have also experienced some of the coldest winters on record. This is not surprising, as weather conditions are expected to become more variable as a result of the greenhouse effect, despite the trend to warmer temperatures. Freak occurrences such as hailstorms and late-spring or even summer frosts

Above: Typical spotting on *Vriesea carinata* from cold conditions.

can occur, in places where little or no frost normally settles.

Fortunately, many bromeliads are surprisingly hardy. Although a number are truly tropical in origin and preference, many are able to survive frosts of -7°C, including a number of more common plants. On the other hand, a variety such as *Guzmania zahnii* 'Variegata' will start showing cold spots when night temperatures drop below 10°C.

Cold sensitivity is variable and plants from the same genus can show very different cold responses, and even plants of the same species can show different sensitivity. Some of this may be due to genetic differences between species, or even between cultivars of the same species. Examples of these intra-genus differences are *Aechmea apocalyptica*, which is quite hardy to several degrees of frost, versus *A. chantinii*, which suffers at less than 10°C; and *Canistropsis billbergioides* 'Persimmon' is at least 2°C hardier than its close relative *C. billbergioides* 'Citron'. Sensitivity is affected by the physical state of the plant, its age and placement; and the length, timing and intensity of the cold period.

Nutrient status is quite critical where temperatures are going to be marginal or damaging to plants. It is well known that with many plant species, bromeliads being no exception, high nitrogen levels in the plant have a negative effect on cold resistance. The reason for this is that nitrogen produces lush growth with weak cell walls which have low resistance to cold (and other problems such as disease).

Conversely, bromeliads that are too low in nitrogen and other nutrients may also be more cold sensitive, as plants weakened by a lack of nutrients have poor growth and an inability to withstand stress. The message here is that bromeliads should be well fed but not overfed, with balanced fertilisers that are not too high in nitrogen.

Two nutrients which are very important in increasing plant resistance to cold are potassium and calcium. Potassium is important as it helps to regulate water flow and pressure in the plant. On cold nights, good water movement in the plant is essential for keeping the warmer soil moisture travelling through the leaves and transferring plant resources to where they are most needed. Calcium is crucial for cell wall strength and a deficiency will lead to weaker cells. Incidentally, high nitrogen levels will disrupt the uptake of both these nutrients, further aggravating the cold problem. Leading up to winter, if your bromeliads need to be fertilised, look for fertilisers that are higher in potassium and preferably have some calcium also.

The timing of fertiliser application is important — applying it late in the autumn is risky if there is a chance of cold damage occurring, and can also lead to a flush of new growth which won't have sufficient time to mature and harden off before winter hits. It is much better to fertilise bromeliads in the spring, with small amounts during summer or early autumn if they need it.

A plant's age has quite an impact on its cold sensitivity. One interesting age-related phenomena I noticed after many seasons of growing bromeliads in marginal climates, was the fact that pups which are attached to a mother plant are much less affected by cold weather than the mother plant itself. In most plants young foliage nearly always suffers much more than mature foliage, and in line with this, pups that have been removed from the mother plant before the cold period suffer damage as expected. Initially, I thought the mother plant's foliage formed a partial cover for the pups; however, after some time I noticed that the effect occurred even with quite large pups that had grown out and above the mother. It wasn't just a case of old weak mothers succumbing first either, as some of them had only recently flowered and still had some years left under normal circumstances. Possibly, bromeliads have evolved so well that in adverse conditions such as cold, the mother plant transfers its resources to the pups to keep them growing well, sacrificing itself in the process. What can be learnt from this is that pups that form in the late autumn, before any expected cold snaps, should probably be left on their mother plants to give them more chance of survival.

The conditions leading up to the cold period over winter have a strong effect on plant resistance to cold damage. When there has been a warm, humid and possibly shady autumn, the plants are likely to have developed rather soft growth, which is in turn more likely to become cold damaged. Unfortunately there is little that can be done in this situation, other than to be more vigilant with cold protection than normal.

Placement of the plants in the garden also has a marked effect on cold sensitivity. Overhanging foliage or proximity to a building reduces the potential for cold damage, and many species that would be cold sensitive in the open can handle quite severe frosts if planted under a tree or shrub. On the other hand, very heavy shrubbery or narrow areas between buildings or fences can actually be detrimental, as poor air movement leads to cold stagnant air pockets, which bromeliads absolutely hate. Therefore, choose locations which benefit from some shelter but still have good air flow.

Planting in a hollow or valley should be avoided at all costs, as cold air settles in hollows where the damage will be much more severe. When choosing spots to plant bromeliads, imagine that the garden is flooded — where water would flow to and settle is where the cold air will also flow and settle. Always try to have the lowest point of the garden free of obstruction so the cold air has somewhere to flow out. Also, if the garden has a stream or dry water course, keep this as clear as possible on the upper banks, to allow the cold air to flow away.

Planting on banks and slopes is recommended for bromeliads. Apart from the improved drainage in these areas, the cold air is less likely to settle in these areas and if they have an aspect that faces the morning or midday sun, the plants will warm more quickly.

Large bodies of water are excellent at reducing cold damage as water holds its temperature much longer than the surrounding air, and so can be used to protect the more sensitive bromeliads. Of course, bromeliads also look great around pools, so this is an excellent solution for gardeners in cooler areas.

Planting among rocks is one of the better ways of keeping bromeliads warm. During the day, the rocks absorb heat from the sun, warming the soil between and under them and warming the plants also. At night, this heat is released slowly, helping to protect the adjacent plants.

Above: Tip dieback from cold wet conditions on *Guzmania zahnii* 'Variegata'.

Good soil drainage is important when selecting sites to plant bromeliads, as they need good drainage in order to form healthy root systems, and a plant with a healthy root system is more capable of withstanding cold temperatures than one of the same species with little or no root system.

There is an assumption that most damage to bromeliads occurs with frosts or freezes. However, the duration of the cold period and the moisture level of the air also has an impact — bromeliads will actually suffer more in the long term from lengthy, cold, wet winters, than from a few short sharp frosts. While a short frost may cause more leaf damage initially, a cold wet winter will cause more plant losses overall, as they eventually succumb to the conditions and develop vase and root rots. Also, these conditions followed by frosts will almost certainly cause many losses as the plants will already be weakened.

Frosts occur most often around the full moon, when the weather is settled, with little wind and clear skies. So keep an eye on the weather forecasts. Contrary to popular belief, a frost may occur at any point below 4.4°C on the weather map. If a frost is predicted, set your alarm for at least half an hour before daybreak and start watering! Don't stop until at least half an hour after daybreak, when the sun starts to warm the plants (or later in shaded areas). Spraying water over plants is a long-established method of preventing frost settling and is surprisingly effective. Frosts can occur well into the spring some years. When this happens the damage is usually most severe, as the plants are often well into their flush of new, softer growth, which can be quite prone to cold damage.

However, if temperatures drop below 0°C, this is known as a freeze and, to be effective, water would need to be applied from the moment that temperatures get below 1°C, which can occur sometime overnight or in the very early hours. A freeze does not necessarily occur in still conditions. So when a freeze is expected, covering the plants with frost cloth, cardboard boxes or straw are really the only practical solutions to protect less-than-hardy plants. It is also a good idea to tip out the vases if a freeze is expected. This will help prevent cold damage which appears as a brown line across the leaves at the water level.

The following groupings should assist gardeners in deciding what to plant from the bromeliads listed in this book. This is not definitive, as I have much more experience with some species in cold gardens than others, and bear in mind that there are always exceptions to every rule. It is not feasible to list every variety and cultivar separately, so some assumptions will have to be made. In most cases I have tried to err on the side of caution. For each grouping, the temperature listed is that which the plants appear to cope with, with little or no damage at that temperature for several hours. However, there may be some damage at lower temperatures. As mentioned above, cold sensitivity is affected by other things which need to be taken into account when deciding what will work for you.

Opposite: Planting among large rocks will help retain heat during winter.

BROMELIADS FOR COLDER CLIMATES

Hardy at -5°C

*Aechmea apocalyptica, A. calyculata, A. 'Cappuccino',
A. caudata, A. 'Covata', A. cylindrata,
A. distichantha, A. gamosepala, A. kertesziae,
A. nudicaulis, A. recurvata, A. triangularis,
A. winkleri*
Billbergia nutans, B. zebrina
Bromelia balansae
Canistropsis billbergioides
*Dyckia brevifolia, D. cinerea, D. fosteriana,
D. ibiramensis, D. marnier-lapostollei,
D. 'Naked Lady'*
Fascicularia bicolor
Nidularium procerum, N. 'Rusty', N. terminale
Ochagavia carnea, O. elegans
Puya alpestris, P. coerulea, P. laxa, P. mirabilis
*Tillandsia recurvata, T. tenuifolia, T. usneoides,
T. utriculata*
*Vriesea corcovadensis, V. flammea, V. philippo-coburgii,
V. vagans*

Hardy at -3°C

Acanthostachys strobilacea
*Aechmea 'Ann Vincent', A. biflora, A. blanchetiana,
A. 'Burgundy', A. callichroma, A. candida,
A. fendleri, A. phanerophlebia, A. pineliana* var.
minuta
Alcantarea geniculata, A. imperialis
Ananas bracteatus
*Billbergia amoena 'Red', B. distachia, B. 'Fantasia',
B. 'Santa Barbara', B. 'Theodore L Mead',
B. vittata, B. 'Windii'*
Cryptbergia 'Mead', C. 'Red Burst'
Neomea 'Strawberry'
*Neoregelia ampullacea, N. 'Apricot Beauty',
N. 'Bea Hanson', N. 'Beta' x 'Magnifica',
N. burle-marxii, N. carcharodon, N. carolinae,
N. carolinae x 'Painted Lady', N. carolinae x
'Vulcan', N. chlorosticta, N. concentrica,
N. 'Crimson Nest', N. cruenta, N. 'Dexters Pride',
N. 'Guinea', N. 'Hearts Blood', N. 'Hojo Rojo',
N. johannis, N. 'Julian Nally', N. marmorata,
N. 'Midnight', N. 'Mottles', N. 'Noble Descent',
N. pineliana, N. 'Sharlock', N. 'Sharlock' x 'Painted
Lady', N. 'Short & Sweet', N. spectabilis,
N. 'Stoplight', N. 'Stormy Weather',
N. tigrina x 'Fireball', N. 'Truly'*
*Nidularium amazonicum, N. antoineanum, N. fulgens,
N. innocentii, N. 'Leprosa', N. 'Lila Rosea',
N. 'Madame Robert Morobe', N. purpureum,
N. 'RaRu', N. rutilans, N. 'Something Special'*
Niduregelia 'Sunrise'
Pitcairnia flammea, P. heterophylla, P. xanthocalyx
*Quesnelia arvensis, Q. humilis, Q. imbricata,
Q. lateralis, Q. liboniana, Q. marmorata*
*Tillandsia argentea, T. capitata, T. 'Creation',
T. cyanea, T. fasciculata, T. filifolia, T. flabellata,
T. imperialis, T. ionantha, T. juncea, T. leiboldiana,
T. secunda, T. somnians, T. streptocarpa, T. stricta,
T. variabilis*
*Vriesea 'Afterglow', V. ensiformis, V. fosteriana,
V. 'Giant' x platynema, V. hieroglyphica, V. 'Mariae',
V. platynema, V. 'Purple Cockatoo', V. simplex*
Wittrockia 'Leopardinum'

Hardy at 0°C

Aechmea aquilega, *A. araneosa*, *A.* 'Big Stuff',
  A. 'Black Jack', *A. caesia*, *A. coelestis*, *A. dealbata*,
  A. 'Exotica Mystique', *A. fasciata*,
  A. 'Fosters Favorite', *A. lueddemanniana*,
  A. mexicana, *A. orlandiana*, *A. pectinata*,
  A. 'Pink Rocket', *A. racinae*, *A.* 'Red Wine',
  A. 'Royal Wine', *A. serrata*, *A. warasii*, *A. weilbachii*
Ananas nanus
Billbergia brasiliensis
Cryptanthus bivittatus, *C. bromelioides*,
  C. 'Carnival de Rio', *C.* 'Cascade', *C.* 'Dusk',
  C. 'It', *C.* 'Red Bird', *C. zonatus*
Guzmania sanguinea, *G. squarrosa*, *G. wittmackii*
Hohenbergia correia-araujoi, *H. stellata*
Neoregelia 'Amazing Grace', *N.* 'Debbie',
  N. 'Fireball', *N.* 'Fireball' x 'Avalon',
  N. 'Fireball' x 'Plutonis', *N.* 'Fosperior Perfection',
  N. 'Gold Fever', *N.* 'Grace', *N.* 'Lila',
  N. 'Maggies Pride', *N. pascoaliana*, *N. princeps*,
  N. 'Purple Star', *N.* 'Sailors Warning',
  N. sarmentosa 'Yellow Bird', *N.* 'Scarlet Charlotte',
  N. 'Tangerine', *N.* 'Ultima'
Orthophytum gurkenii, *O. saxicola*
Pitcairnia atrorubens, *P. tabuliformis*
Tillandsia caput-medusae, *T. complanata*, *T. crocata*,
  T. deppeana, *T. multicaulis*, *T. tectorum*, *T. viridiflora*,
  T. xerographica
Vriesea carinata, *V. glutinosa*, *V. guttata*, *V. inflata*,
  V. 'Sanderiana'

Hardy at +5°C or higher

Aechmea chantinii, *A.* 'Fosters Favorite Favorite',
  A. dichlamydea var. *trinitensis*, *A.* 'Little Harve',
  A. spectabilis
Ananas comosus
Billbergia pyramidalis
Guzmania 'Amaranth', *G. bismarckii*,
  G. 'Cherry Smash', *G.* 'Claret', *G. conifera*,
  G. 'Decora', *G. lingulata*, *G.* 'Mandarine',
  G. monostachia, *G.* 'Omer Morobe',
  G. 'Orangeade', *G.* 'Ostara', *G.* 'Pax', *G. zahnii*
Vriesea maxoniana, *V.* 'Plantation Pride',
  V. 'Poelmanii', *V. splendens*, *V.* 'Splenriet',
  V. zamorensis

Although low temperatures are of most concern to bromeliad growers, high temperatures can also sometimes be a problem. There are a number of species native to higher altitudes that suffer badly when cultivated in the hotter and more humid climates of the lower altitudes. Excess temperatures can also cause leaf scorching, particularly on varieties with thin leaves.

Some species with coloured foliage from genera such as *Neoregelia* often need warm daytime temperatures followed by cool nights to develop their best colouration — another factor to take into account.

CLIMATE ZONES

Many nurseries now give an indication of how hardy their plants will be, and this hardiness may be indicated by reference to climate zone maps or to temperature ranges (see temperature conversion chart on p 195).

Where climate zone maps are used, these need to be treated with caution. Firstly, be aware that microclimates make a major difference in some areas — a region that is considered cold may have a small pocket which resides next to a lake, for example. Another common occurrence is for larger cities to have their own climate, generally several degrees higher than the surrounding countryside. Each country also has its own system of dividing themselves into climate zones, and these systems may be based on different parameters.

In the United States, zone 11 is the warmest, and these warm temperatures are only achieved in Hawaii and Puerto Rico. Here, the annual average minimum temperature will be more than 4.5°C, so all bromeliads will grow well there, except those that need the cold to do well.

Zone 10b includes such areas as southern Florida, with a minimum temperature range of 1.7–4.4°C. In practise, all bromeliads will grow there; however, some damage may occur in the coldest winters on the most tropical plants.

In Zone 10a, which includes parts of Florida and southern California around the Gulf of Mexico and the Pacific coast, only those bromeliads that can handle light frosts should be grown outdoors without protection.

Minimum winter temperatures average -1.1–1.6°C.

Zone 9b covers southern central and coastal Florida, the edge of southern Texas and the rest of California along the Pacific coast and inland from the Gulf of Mexico. This zone can experience frosts down to -3.8°C, so the range of bromeliads that can be grown there is more limited.

Zone 9a covers most of the rest of California, except the higher altitudes and the northern tip, the south-western corner of Arizona, the rest of central Florida, the south of Louisiana and about the lower quarter of Texas. This zone can experience quite heavy frosts, down to -6.6°C, although these are not that common. In colder areas than these only the toughest bromeliads will survive.

In Europe, zone 10 is the warmest and covers the coasts of Spain and Portugal, including cities such as Lisbon, Valencia, Seville, Barcelona and La Coruna. Zone 10 also includes Italy from Naples south (including Sicily), Corsica and southern Greece. Here, many bromeliads will grow well, but only those that can handle light frosts should be grown outdoors without protection.

Zone 9 covers virtually all of the rest of the Mediterranean coastline and extends up the Atlantic coast of France and the south-western coasts of Ireland and Britain. It also goes inland into Spain and Italy for some distance. This zone can experience quite heavy frosts down to -6°C, although right on the coast itself the frosts may be less severe. The range of bromeliads that can be grown in zone 9 is fairly limited, but there are still a number of species and hybrids which are suitable.

In Australia, most of the continent can be used for growing bromeliads, with the limiting factor in the interior being the lack of water. However, there are cold zones, where bromeliads will struggle. Only the hardiest bromeliads that can handle temperatures below -5°C can be grown in the high country of Tasmania and the mountain ranges of New South Wales, Queensland and Victoria.

Most of the southern half of Australia, except the coast, is suitable for bromeliads that can handle frosts down to -5°C. For these coastal areas and for most of the northern half of the continent, most bromeliads will flourish, except the truly tropical types. These can only be grown successfully

Above: This new planting of *Neoregelia* 'Mottles' pups is being supported by temporary stakes.

outdoors in the more tropical zone, which covers some of the Queensland coast, Western Australia north of Shark Bay and the top end. Any bromeliads can be grown in these areas, except those that need the cold to do well.

In New Zealand, all except the most tropical bromeliads will flourish from Kaitaia in the north to Kerikeri. Slight frost hardiness is needed for those bromeliads planted in the area from Dargaville to Auckland. South Auckland, the east coast to Blenheim and the west coast to Hokitika can grow bromeliads that can take moderate frosts. Inland or south from these areas, only the hardiest bromeliads will do well.

PLANTING

There are various planting techniques that will increase the chance of survival and success of newly planted bromeliads. In general, space the plants at least one plant width apart. This allows at least one generation of pups to develop before you need to consider thinning out or transplanting. However, if the plant is not full size, for example a small *Vriesea hieroglyphica* or *Alcantarea imperialis*, then you will need to allow more space (a full-size *A. imperialis* can have a span of 1.5 m). If you need to fill the gaps with smaller bromeliads or low groundcover plants, such as *Scleranthus* or Mondo grass.

Most bromeliads need free-draining soil. A good test for this is to pour a litre of water on a small depression in the soil. If it disappears almost immediately, it is free draining.

If the water sits on the surface and takes some minutes to drain, it can be considered a heavy soil. If it is a heavy soil or clay or does not drain well, then a layer of free-draining material such as composted bark, fibrous compost or similar should be placed over the top — most bromeliads only need a layer 5–12 cm deep. A hole the width of the pot is all that is required when digging into this type of soil.

It is an advantage, but not absolutely necessary, for the soil to have good nutrient levels. Bromeliads will feed off matter that falls into the cups, but will grow better if the soil has some nutrients also. However, avoid products that contain mushroom compost or animal manure though, as they can provide too much of a good thing.

When planting, simply tip the plant upside down and remove from the pot. Most of the potting mix should come with the root ball, but if the plant has very few roots, then just tip the loose potting mix into the hole. Place the plant at the height it was in the pot. If it is unstable, just wedge some small stones around the base, and it will gradually stabilise itself as pups develop.

Give the plant a good watering as soon as it is planted to top up the cup and help it get over the trauma of travel and handling. A light sprinkling of water every few days after planting is also beneficial until the plant is settled in its new environment. A little bit of extra shade for the first few days also helps.

It is normal for one or two of the lower leaves to go yellow or die back some weeks after planting. This is the plant's response to handling and the new environment. Sometimes the root system may die back also, but the plant will send new roots out if its new situation is favourable. Younger plants are more able to produce new roots than plants which have already flowered, so keep this in mind when purchasing bromeliads.

If the plant begins to yellow, or scorch marks appear on the leaf, this is much more serious and indicates that its new situation is not to its liking. As soon as this yellowing or scorching is noticed, move the plant to a shadier spot, as excess light is the most likely cause of this symptom.

WATERING

Despite the fact that many bromeliads come from wet areas, problems can result from overwatering in heavy soil or poorly aerated potting mix. Overwatering can be very damaging to bromeliads as the root systems need plenty of oxygen to keep the plants growing well. Plants grown in waterlogged soils fail to develop healthy feeding roots, and what roots they do have are quickly lost to rot. This is why many of the potting mixes recommended for these plants are very free draining. But even with free-draining soils and potting mixes, waterlogging can still occur. As a rough guide, allow the surface of the soil or mix to dry out before watering again, at least to a depth of a couple of millimetres.

Most bromeliads can withstand extended dry periods and prolonged wet conditions if grown in suitable soil or potting mix. However, over time, these extreme conditions will be detrimental, showing up as slower growth, withering of leaves, quilling of foliage (when the top leaves stick together into a narrow 'quill' or cigar-shaped structure), or increased levels of root and leaf disease.

In most regions, there is sufficient rainfall to cater to all but the most moisture-dependent bromeliads for most of the year, without needing to irrigate. Watch the plants though — a general rule is the plants that need the most shade will also need the most water, while the plants that prefer full sun are better adapted to withstanding drought conditions. As always, there are many exceptions to this. However, based on this guide, during the heat of the summer, the shade-loving plants will probably need a good overhead water at least once a week if there has been no rain. The most sun-loving types will need a good drenching about once every 2–3 weeks; and those that like partial shade should be watered at least every 1–2 weeks.

During winter, watering the shade-loving plants every 3–4 weeks is sufficient; with the sun-loving plants probably not needing any watering for at least six weeks at a time. Note that care is needed over winter with *Pitcairnia* species, as although their habitat is often damp creek banks, they usually do best when they can have a semi-dormant, dry period for several months during winter.

Where possible water soil- or pot-grown bromeliads over the foliage and allow plenty of water to run into the soil or potting mix in order to keep the root system moist. A moist root system will aid plant growth as it can continue to draw up the water and nutrients.

Bromeliads grown in pots will need watering more frequently, as there is much less of a buffer of moist soil available to the plants. In summer, water may be needed every 2–3 days, and terrestrial types such as *Cryptanthus*, *Dyckia*, *Orthophytum* and *Pitcairnia*, may need watering daily as their normally extensive root systems are constrained by the pots, and they don't have the natural water reservoir that many of the other genera have. A peculiarity with many of these terrestrial types is that they sometimes need to be watered from below, by soaking the pot. This is because they form such tight clumps that they cover the surface when potted.

Bromeliads grown as epiphytes also have different requirements. These rely entirely on water supplied by rainfall or hand watering and there is usually little or no buffer of water for the root system to draw from. In summer, these plants will begin to suffer after a few days without moisture. However, unlike other plants, which visibly wilt when thirsty, this can often go unnoticed, as they can suffer lengthy dry periods without visible changes — rest assured that the plants will be suffering and growth will be reduced.

Most people visualise *Tillandsia* as dry-growing, sun-loving epiphytes. That view has been aggravated by the common technique of gluing *Tillandsia* species to tacky ornaments and refrigerator magnets, with the implication that these 'air plants' can survive on air alone. Nothing could be further from the truth. Those species with the heaviest covering of peltate (fuzzy) scales will survive dry conditions best, but they still need ample water on a regular basis to continue growing and flowering to their best. In summer, they will need watering every 3–4 days, with a good soaking each time, while in dry climates this is needed once every 1–2 days. In cool or humid climates the plants can have less water. If they are mounted on small pieces of wood or similar, they can be dunked under water for up to half an hour. It is best not to water these after midday in winter, as the plants need to be quite dry by nightfall when they absorb carbon dioxide.

Tank-type bromeliads can absorb water through the leaves as well as the roots, so if water supplies are limited,

Above: Poor-quality water high in calcium and other salts has marked the flower bracts of this otherwise lovely *Nidularium* 'Madame Robert Morobe'.

as is the case in many country or coastal areas over summer, just a light sprinkling over the foliage is enough to keep them going until the next rainfall. This makes these bromeliads ideal for areas where water conservation is needed. Do avoid watering *Neoregelia* and *Guzmania sanguinea* into the vase during their flowering period though, as the water can quickly turn vile and smelly with all the rotting petals and bracts. If they cannot be kept dry and already have smelly water in them, try to rinse this out with fresh water at least each week or tip the plants out.

Water quality is very important for bromeliads; in fact, they actually need higher water quality that what people normally drink! As these plants take up both water and nutrients through the leaves, any impurities in the water supply can disrupt this process and damage the plants. The easiest way to determine early if your water is harming your bromeliads, is to observe whether any white deposits form on the leaves, particularly around the vase. These may be due to high alkalinity, caused by too much calcium or magnesium carbonate in the water. Another possible cause is high salt levels. In either case, a change to clean water is essential, and this is best obtained by collecting rainwater (unless copper gutters are in use) or by taking water from a purifier, of the type used in many offices and homes these days. Let it warm up to room temperature before using.

FEEDING

The subject of fertilising bromeliads is one of the most controversial, and every grower has their own theories which they swear by. Feeding advice ranges from 'no fertiliser at all', to 'apply liquid fertiliser only' and 'feed well for best results'. Confused? I am not surprised. However, there are many good reasons for all this apparently conflicting advice. With the vast range of bromeliads and the enormous variety of habitats they come from, it follows that nutrient requirements for each species will also be different. Also, different growing methods, such as watering practices and soil type, will produce very different results even when applying the same amount of fertiliser. To further complicate matters, what may look like an attractive vigorous plant to one person, may look overgrown and out of character to another. Or a highly coloured squat little plant may look stunning to one person, but simply looks stressed and undernourished to the other.

However, there is no doubt that bromeliads need fertiliser. Without nutrients, even the most hardy of plants will eventually curl up its toes and die. With adequate nutrition, bromeliads can be grown to their best.

One of the features of bromeliads that has led many people to consider they don't need feeding is their ability to take up significant quantities of nutrients through the leaves. Indeed, most bromeliads live in environments that are very low in nutrients, such as sandy soils, rock faces, as epiphytes and even in swampy soils. As a result, they have adapted to become very adept at scavenging for nutrients and can survive on very little. But that is the key point — they survive. Gardeners want their plants to do more than just survive, they want them to flourish and look fantastic, which is why we fertilise bromeliads.

The more difficult question about fertiliser is what type to use and how much to apply. This is where the arguments get more convoluted and where we should understand the principle that each plant has different requirements. Fortunately though, we can roughly group the plants according to their needs.

Nearly all the soft green-leaved types of bromeliad respond well to frequent feeding at reasonably high rates. Examples of these are *Aechmea gamosepala*, *Billbergia pyramidalis*, *Canistropsis billbergioides*, *Guzmania wittmackii*, *Neoregelia carolinae*, *Nidularium rutilans*, *Pitcairnia tabuliformis*, *Tillandsia multicaulis* and *Vriesea hieroglyphica*. Also included in this group are the soft, coloured-leaved plants like *Aechmea* 'Royal Wine' and *A.* 'Fosters Favorite'.

For these plants, a teaspoon of 9–12 month slow-release fertiliser applied around the base each spring is ideal. Larger plants from this group will need proportionally more, for example a 1 m-wide *Vriesea hieroglyphica* can take up to a tablespoon of slow-release fertiliser. These plants also respond well to foliar feeding, which can be done as often as weekly if you have the time. This becomes more important when the plants are grown as epiphytes, as the root system is not as capable of feeding the plant.

Overfeeding these plants will result in strappy leaves that bend easily and are not as resistant to cold or wind. Underfeeding will result in harder leaves, but smaller and less dramatic flower spikes, as well as smaller plants, which may be light green or even yellow in appearance

Below: The bromeliad on the right has been well fertilised. The same species on the left is grown in the same area, but fed much less.

and much less resistant to disease. Contrary to popular belief, feeding vivid-coloured plants such as *Neoregelia carolinae* well will not necessarily result in loss of leaf colour. Certainly if the fertiliser is high in nitrogen and phosphorus this may occur, but plants fertilised with a balanced fertiliser will keep their colour and, in fact, if they are grown in good light, proper fertilisation will actually enhance leaf colour.

On the other hand, the neoregelias with tough leathery leaves and heavy mottling or banding will need to be treated quite differently. As a rough rule of thumb with the rest of this genus, the tougher and more highly coloured the foliage, the less fertiliser should be applied, taking into account the eventual size of the plants. For example, a potted *Neoregelia ampullacea* will need no more than half a teaspoon of slow-release fertiliser every second year to keep it looking its best, while a large *N. pascoaliana* may need 1–2 teaspoons each year to achieve the same result.

Apart from the soft green-leaved types, most *Billbergia* should be dealt with quite harshly when it comes to nutrition. They are such vigorous growers and such opportunists that they will go green and grow like cabbages if too much nutrient is supplied. These are best kept away from fertile soils, preferably placed in trees or pots to restrain the root systems and be fed very little. No more than half a teaspoon of slow-release fertiliser applied every second spring is needed. As an alternative, liquid fertiliser is useful to control growth and manage leaf colour as the rates and timing can be adjusted according to how stressed the plants look. Billbergias will first show severe nutrient stress as dying leaf tips.

Terrestrial bromeliads such as *Ananas*, *Cryptanthus*, *Orthophytum*, *Puya* and *Pitcairnia* are actually quite heavy feeders. These do best in a rich soil with a high humus content and a pH that is closer to neutral — dolomite or lime may be needed to raise the pH to a suitable level. The amount of dolomite or lime to apply depends on the natural soil pH and the amount of calcium and magnesium already in the soil — the best way to determine this is to get a soil test taken by an analytical laboratory. The smaller *Orthophytum* and *Cryptanthus* species need about 1 teaspoon per plant of slow-release fertiliser in spring,

Above: *Billbergia* 'Milagro' is a good example of the type of plant that should be fed sparingly to keep the intense colour.

while the larger *Ananas* and *Puya* can take up to 1 tablespoon per plant.

Semi-terrestrial plants such as the larger *Quesnelia* and *Portea* along with most of the larger *Aechmea*, are best fed quite well when they are young, at similar rates to *Ananas*. However, it is a good idea to reduce feeding when they are approaching maturity to allow them to harden off, making them more hardy, with better leaf colour and more likely to flower.

This also applies to a number of the larger *Neoregelia*, but in particular to the large *Vriesea* and *Alcantarea*, which can be grown quite quickly in their earlier years by generous application of fertiliser. For example, a pair of *Aechmea imperialis* 'Rubra' that I grew in two very large pots, were fed with 4 tablespoons each of 9–12 month slow-release fertiliser up to four years of age. In year five they were given half this amount and none from then on. As a result the pair of them grew very vigorously for the next three years, attaining more leaf colour each year as the fertiliser effect slowly wore off. In three years they grew from 50 cm-high plants to 1.2 m-high plants with great shape and glorious colour.

What is the best way of feeding bromeliads? As a generalisation, except for plants grown as epiphytes where application of solid fertilisers is impractical, solid fertilisers applied to the soil or potting mix will produce plants which have thicker, stronger leaves with deeper colour than those which are fed exclusively on foliar-applied fertilisers. Although the most commonly grown bromeliads are found in the wild as epiphytes, all those that are capable of forming roots in the soil or potting mix are also quite capable of taking their entire nutrient requirements through the root system.

However, many people like to use liquid feeds to keep their plants in top form. Liquid feeding is a useful technique for topping up nutrient levels on all bromeliads and particularly as they take up nutrients this way so effectively. It is very useful where plants are under some stress, for example in the heat of summer or if their root systems have suffered some injury. Liquid feeding is also a useful filler when the next application of slow-release fertilisers is not planned for some time. Of course liquid feeding is essential when growing bromeliads as epiphytes.

The pH level for liquid feeding most bromeliads should be about 5–6.5. A fairly dilute solution is recommended, particularly for thin-leaved types, as these can easily burn. To be on the safe side, the liquid feed strength for bromeliads is best kept at an Electrical Conductivity (EC) level of 1.0–1.4 mS/cm (CF 10–14). Electrical Conductivity is a measure of the amount of nutrient salts in solution and can be measured using EC or CF meters, which are available from hydroponic suppliers. For most liquid fertilisers, this equates to approximately 1–1.5 ml per litre of water, and for most powder-type fertiliser concentrates, this is about 1 g per litre of water, or 1 teaspoon per 5 litres of water. For bromeliads that are less sensitive, or those that need more fertiliser, the strength

can be increased up to 2 g per litre of water, but this will need to be applied with care, as the risk of burning is much greater. This strength is actually quite low compared to that used for many other plants, but needs to be sufficiently low to avoid burning in even the most sensitive bromeliads.

Liquid feeds are best applied over the complete leaf area of the plants as this whole area is able to take up nutrients, although the tank is where most nutrient absorption will take place. Some people advise washing the leaves with fresh water after feeding; however, this will remove any nutrients that are left. It is better to be on the safe side and use less fertiliser less often, then washing off is not necessary. However, over time, nutrient salts can build up in the vase of tank-type bromeliads and this can cause burning of the inner leaves, so it is advisable to flush out the tank after 3–4 nutrient applications.

Any liquid feeding should preferably be done in the early morning or late evening to avoid the potential for leaf

Below: Severe burning caused by foliar fertiliser that has been applied too concentrated.

burn. Cloudy days are best, as this allows the nutrients to stay in liquid form on the leaf for as long as possible, giving the plants their best chance of taking up the nutrients.

Unless bromeliads are grown in tropical areas or greenhouses, most active growth will take place over the three warmer seasons — spring until autumn. During winter the plants will grow very little. Therefore there is no point in supplying lots of fertiliser during winter, unless the soil is completely devoid of nutrients. In fact, feeding bromeliads just before or during winter can lead to soft growth, which is more prone to cold damage. The only time this should be done is if winter temperatures are expected to remain above 10–12°C at all times or in a heated greenhouse, as growth will continue, although more slowly than in the other seasons due to the lower light levels.

For solid fertilisers, in particular slow-release pellets, spring is without doubt the best time of year to apply. This gives the plants a boost of nutrients during a good growing period, and sets them up well to cope with the heat of summer. Liquid fertilisers can be applied as often as practical, and most large commercial nurseries now apply nutrients in every irrigation. In the home garden, this is not usually practical, but try to apply the fertiliser as often as you can over the main growing period.

When considering fertilising your garden, you must also take into account the natural fertility of your soil and the way in which your bromeliads are being grown. If the soil is low in nutrients, such as a light sandy soil, or a heavy clay from which the roots are not easily able to take nutrients, then annual side dressing with fertilisers is beneficial. If the soil is fertile, then very little if any fertilisers will be needed. In larger metropolitan areas it is quite common for smaller gardens to have soil brought in as a pre-made compost. In these soils, the nutrient levels are usually quite high and little fertilisers are needed.

Where plants are grown in more adverse situations, like rock gardens, then annual fertiliser application can be beneficial for producing top-quality plants. For potted plants, it is reasonable to assume that the nutrients contained in the potting mix are sufficient for the first year of growth. However, unless the plants are potted into new mix, after the first year fertilisers should be applied annually.

Bromeliads being grown as epiphytes are a special case. As there are normally no nutrient reserves available, these plants must be fed on a regular basis. If the plants are in a well-developed garden, they may get sufficient from bird droppings, leaves, insects and rain. However, in a poorly vegetated garden, there may be much less detritus available to fall into the epiphytes and regular feeding is essential. Similarly, if the epiphytes are grown indoors or under the eaves of a building, virtually all the nutrients will have to be supplied by the gardener.

Plants of a particular species or cultivar grown in low light will require less fertiliser than the same plant grown in more light. As the light level increases, so does the rate of photosynthesis and therefore the need for nutrients. In fact, one of the best ways of making a plant more sun tolerant is gradually increasing the amount of fertiliser applied once it has been planted in the higher light area.

When selecting a fertiliser for bromeliads, the most important thing to look for is its NPK ratio. This is the ratio of the three most important nutrients that every plant requires: Nitrogen (N), Phosphorus (P) and Potassium (K). (Be aware, however, that in some countries, the P and K on the packet doesn't refer to Phosphorus and Potassium, but rather their oxides, which may be listed further down as P2O5 and K2O. The oxides have less of each element by weight, so multiply P2O5 by 0.44 to get P and K2O by 0.83 to get K.)

Irrespective of whether you are choosing liquid or solid fertilisers, it should have an NPK ratio close to what is considered ideal for bromeliads. Experience and experimentation has shown that bromeliads have considerable need for potassium and less for phosphorus and nitrogen. Therefore, look for fertilisers that have the K level higher than N, up to twice as high. N in turn should be at least twice P. As an example, a ratio of NPK of 5:2:7 would be satisfactory.

It is often difficult to obtain fertilisers with high potassium, as most pre-mixed fertilisers tend to have potassium equal to or slightly lower than nitrogen, which most plants prefer. It pays to look out for fertilisers that are advertised specifically as 'High K' or 'Low N'.

If you want to get more precise, the nutrient ratio can be varied over the year and according to the age and type of plant. For example, green-leaved bromeliads can take more nitrogen for vigorous growth, while red-leaved bromeliads usually prefer more potassium for best leaf colour. Older plants will need less nitrogen than younger plants; and fertilisers applied in summer can have more nitrogen than those applied in winter.

Avoid using fertilisers in their raw form, such as potassium sulphate or calcium nitrate. These are very concentrated and if not applied correctly, can burn the foliage or roots. It is better to choose slow-release fertiliser pellets which are much safer to use, and for bromeliads the 9–12 month nutrient release pellets are probably the most practical.

If you prefer to use organic or natural fertilisers, it is still important that they have a high potassium to nitrogen ratio. Generally, fish- or seaweed-based products are best, but watch out for leaf burn, as this is more likely with the oilier liquids such as fish fertiliser. Most animal manures, including blood and bone, are too high in nitrogen and phosphorus to be useful. An exception is sheep manure, which can have a reasonably high level of potassium.

FLOWERING

When a bromeliad is mature, it may come into flower. The flowering time for bromeliads is never certain, but usually occurs when the plant is a certain size and during a particular season. The flowering season is different for every species, and there are different bromeliads in flower every month of the year. No one season is any better than another for flowering of this family.

Some bromeliads are very reluctant to flower, even when full size. This is due to a number of factors but most commonly temperature. In commercial nurseries, natural flowering can't always be relied on, so a trick is used to make the plants flower. This trick was discovered in the pineapple plantations of the Azores in 1874, when some observant person noted that whenever crop stubble was burnt off in the paddocks surrounding the pineapple fields, the pineapple plants would fruit en masse some months after the smoke cleared. Eventually it was discovered that the ethylene in the smoke caused these plants to flower. Once this was known, the technique was tried with success on other bromeliads. Now, modern bromeliad nurseries use products which produce ethylene gas in the vases of the bromeliad plants. These cause no long-term effect on the plant other than triggering it to flower.

However, sometimes commercial nurseries will use ethylene treatments when plants are too young, and in this case, they may not flower, or will have deformed flower stems. A young plant forced into flower may also fail to produce pups and will gradually die. With experience, a gardener can learn to avoid these plants when buying bromeliads.

The home gardener can also take advantage of this unique ability of bromeliads to flower in response to ethylene. Empty out and cover the chosen plant with a paper bag (not plastic as this can cause sweating and heat damage). Inside the bag, place a banana skin or apple core and leave it there for about 5–7 days. If the plant is potted, then drain the water from its cup and use a clear plastic bag, but keep the plant in full shade until the bag is removed again. The ethylene given off by the fruit is usually sufficient to induce the plant to flower. Depending on the variety, flowering should occur 10–16 weeks later.

For large numbers of plants, or where more dependable success rates are needed, ethylene-producing chemicals can be used. There are a range of options, including calcium carbide, acetylene, and commercial products such as Ethrel™ or Florel™.

SOIL TYPE & POTTING MIX

Bromeliads are reasonably fussy about their soil, and apart from the fact that many are epiphytes with very specific requirements, even the terrestrials need certain soil conditions to do well. They need soils that usually have satisfactory drainage; and specific acidity and nutrient characteristics which can be found in volcanic loam, sandy soils near the coast, light river silt and soils with high organic matter such as peat loam or thick leaf litter.

Satisfactory drainage is critical for nearly all bromeliads, but soils with poor drainage can often be improved by mixing in pumice, sand or bark, and other organic materials such as peat. Bromeliads thrive in free-draining soils with a high proportion of organic matter — compost is useful here.

Most of the epiphytic and tank-forming bromeliads prefer soils with reasonably low pH. A soil pH level of 5.5–6.5 is generally satisfactory although levels slightly outside this range should not cause problems. Incorporation of acidic organic products such as peat and composted bark can assist in reducing pH. Terrestrial bromeliads, on the other hand, tend to prefer a neutral to slightly alkaline soil pH.

When it comes to potting mixes for bromeliads, every type of ingredient known is available. Some people prefer peat, others bark or coir fibre as the base ingredient. Some add polystyrene chips, others pumice, gravel, river grit or sand. Most people who grow bromeliads on a small scale simply use bagged mixes from their nearest garden centre.

Despite all these incredibly diverse potting mixes, most people can grow fantastic bromeliads in any of them, because for some plants virtually any growing medium is suitable, provided the growing conditions are made to suit the different characteristics of each mix. The mix you use should be tailored to match the plant you are growing and your individual watering habits, lighting and general growing conditions.

Each group of bromeliads does have different requirements. Terrestrial bromeliads such as *Cryptanthus*, *Dyckia*, *Orthophytum*, *Pitcairnia* and *Puya* have large and well-developed root systems which need adequate water and often grow in neutral or slightly alkaline soils. These bromeliads prefer the heavier potting mixes that are sold in many garden centres for general house or patio plant use.

Tank-type epiphytes or terrestrial bromeliads have less well-developed root systems and these plants prefer very free-draining potting mix which is on the acid side. If purchasing potting mix straight from a garden centre, try blending an orchid mix with a general house-plant mix.

Highly epiphytic plants, if they are to be grown in pots at all, will need a very free-draining media. Pure orchid mix is the best for these types. Be aware though, that even the most open mix will be too much for some epiphytes, which can only be grown with nothing around their base.

Many gardeners like to make up their own mix, using the following guidelines. However, when selecting the raw ingredients, there are a few things to be aware of. The main one is to use natural products that have been well composted. Natural products that have not been composted, such as tree-fern fibre, pine bark or similar, will use up all the available nitrogen from the potting mix as they gradually compost, leaving your plants starved of nitrogen. Also avoid any products which are too fine, such as fine peat or dusty pumice. These can quickly clog the potting mix, making it totally unsuitable. Be careful with some products that may have undesirable side effects, such as coir fibre which has not been properly leached. The high salt content in this product is very toxic to bromeliads and should only be used if it has been properly leached by the manufacturer.

When potting up pups or seedlings, there is no point feeding a lot of fertiliser straight away, as the new root system will not have formed and the unused nutrients can build up to toxic levels or create a haven for moss and

Product	Effect on pH	Effect on Drainage
Composted bark fines	Acid	Reduces
Composted bark chips	Acid	Increases
Pumice	Neutral	Increases
Peat	Acid	Reduces
Tree-fern fibre	Acid	Increases
Perlite	Neutral	Increases
Sphagnum	Acid	Reduces
Gravel	Neutral	Increases
Limestone	Alkaline	Increases
Sand	Neutral	Varies

algae. It is better to wait until the plants are putting out new white roots and then fertilise. Until the new roots have formed, the pups or seedlings can be fed with liquid feed, which will help the plant develop its root system.

PESTS, DISEASES & DISORDERS

Compared to many other garden plants, bromeliads are quite pest- and disease-resistant, and those that do occur usually only cause minor or seasonal damage.

The plant's environment is the most important factor in avoiding or reducing pest and disease problems. Most of the fungi that attack bromeliads rely on poor air movement and humid conditions to establish, so avoiding planting in poorly ventilated rooms or in dank narrow areas in the garden is a good first step in preventing fungal diseases. Avoiding overcrowding will also help to keep good air movement around the plants. Plants that are too overcrowded and don't get a regular washing of water over the leaves are also more likely to suffer from scale and mealybug. However, even with a good environment and despite best intentions, pests and diseases can sometimes become established.

Aphids

Aphids can be a problem on emerging flower stems during spring and summer. If they build up to very high levels, they can cause deformities to the flower spikes of *Pitcairnia*, *Aechmea*, some *Guzmania* and *Vriesea*. This is rare though, and in a garden situation aphids usually prefer other plant species. If they do become a problem, spraying the flowers with a solution of dishwashing liquid at 1 teaspoon per litre of water deals with them effectively, or alternatively, for a quick fix, a light spray with flyspray is very effective. Be careful with flyspray though, as too much on the leaves will cause burning.

Earwigs

Earwigs can inhabit bromeliads in large numbers, particularly in large bromeliads grown as epiphytes. They cause damage by chewing on the emerging stem or feeding on the leaves which gives a ragged appearance. Earwigs are easily recognisable by their pincers at the end of their abdomen; they are dark reddish brown, with light brown legs. They are primarily nocturnal scavengers, eating dead insects and decomposing plant materials, so removing debris helps control earwigs. Insecticide treatment should be concentrated around pots, paths and crevices. A sprinkling of diatomaceous earth dust will work. Another effective technique is placing a crumpled-up piece of newspaper near the plants overnight. The earwigs will shelter here and in the morning, just crush or burn, with pleasure!

Footrot

Footrot disease is caused by *Fusarium oxysporum*, and this is seen rotting at the base. If the plant is cut through just below the growing point, the normally white area will be coloured brown. This disease is aggravated by high temperatures, weak growth, root damage caused by something like overwatering and dense planting. If it

Below: Footrot has completely destroyed the base of this *Vriesea*, with only a few highly stressed upper leaves surviving till the end.

becomes a problem, it can be prevented by drenching the soil or potting mix with 250 g per 1 m³ Terrazole and 250 g per 1 m³ Bavistin.

Leaf spotting

Leaf spotting disease is caused by *Fusarium sacchari* var. *elongatum*. This is seen as light, transparent flecks on the leaves, which turn yellow then brown, and in some cases the outer leaves will rot off at the base. This disease is prevented by avoiding excessive humidity and making sure that plants are not too dense, as the disease thrives on poor air circulation. It can be controlled by spraying with 1 g per 1 litre Topsin or Cleary's 3336.

Brown flecks on the leaves can also be caused by slow growth and high humidity, and shows up as damage at the boundary of water and air in the vase of the plant gradually growing out.

Mosquitoes

Although mosquitoes don't damage bromeliads, they are certainly a pest for humans, and one of the main reasons some people refuse to grow them.

Although bromeliads are often blamed for mosquito problems, most species breed elsewhere. The main group of mosquitoes to breed in bromeliads are all from the

Below: Leaf spotting disease on a young *Vriesea* hybrid.

genus *Wyeomyia*, and are known as the bromeliad mosquito for that reason. These small insects are not found in many countries. The more common species of mosquitoes prefer other breeding grounds, such as ponds, shallow puddles, blocked gutters and similar environments. Salt-marsh mosquitoes prefer brackish or salty water and are almost never found in bromeliads.

Mosquitoes will however take advantage of the habitat provided by bromeliads. Chemical control is an option where there are health concerns, such as areas with dengue fever or similar, but chemical spraying should be the last option, as this will disrupt the natural ecosystem that develops around and in the plants. This natural ecosystem is the first and best line of defence against mosquitoes, and in fact wild or untouched bromeliads have very few mosquitos in them.

One of the best non-chemical actions that can be taken is to periodically empty or flush out the vases of your bromeliads. If the collection is large or time is limited, concentrate on older, flowering *Neoregelia*, as the rotting flowers in the vase supplies food for mosquito larvae. It also helps to twist and pull out the old flower spike of the neoregelias after flowering, as this removes the food source completely.

One of the most effective controls for mosquitoes, and incidentally slugs and snails also, is coffee grounds. Sprinkle the bromeliads liberally with spent coffee grounds and the caffeine will quickly kill both the larvae and any other soft-bodied creature that comes into contact with the water. Tobacco has much the same effect.

Quilling

Drought stress is indicated on many bromeliads by a phenomenon called quilling. This is when the inner leaves of the plant or pup are stuck together, forming a quill effect. Some species are very sensitive to this, in particular many *Guzmania* and *Vriesea*, but also some *Neoregelia* and *Aechmea*. Quilling usually occurs in plants grown in a dry environment, and may indicate that the soil or potting mix is too dry, but usually it reflects low humidity.

Quilling can be overcome by carefully separating the leaves from each other by hand. If this is not possible, in

Above: The inner leaves of this *Guzmania* hybrid have quilled quite badly.

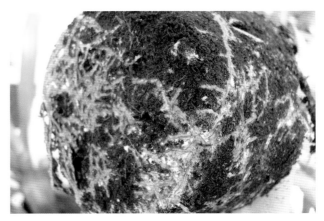

Above: The fluffy white masses surrounding the roots are root mealybug.

bad cases, then the plants can be drenched with a solution of 1 teaspoon of dishwashing liquid to 4 litres of water. Rinse the plants with a strong stream of fresh water within a couple of hours after treatment and this will help loosen the leaves from each other.

Root mealybug

Root mealybug is a relatively common problem for bromeliads. I have found that these nasty little bugs are more prevalent on some species than on others, in particular, *Billbergia* and *Cryptbergia*, with some of the more epiphytic *Aechmea* also being susceptible. Root mealybug form colonies attached to the root system, covered in a protective white fluffy substance, making them relatively hard to kill. They tend to be more prevalent in pots than in the soil.

Where there is only a plant or two affected, take these well away from the rest of the collection, as these little pests can transfer quite easily from plant to plant. If only one or two plants are affected, it may be most efficient to simply strip the root system away completely, throw away the pot and mix and treat them as unrooted pups. Systemic insecticides designed for use on these pests is about the only way to eliminate them on a large scale, although insect growth regulator chemicals used for scale may be effective.

Scale

Scale insects can settle and multiply on the top or underside of leaves, although they build up most rapidly on the underside. They can cause round yellow leaf markings which detract greatly from the appearance of the plants, but they often go unnoticed until the populations have grown to a serious stage. Plants that are grown outside usually have little trouble with scale, unless they are grown in dry zones of the garden, or the clumps are very dense. Indoor plants have much more trouble, partly due to less frequent water movement over the leaves, which washes the juvenile crawlers off, but also partly due to the lack of natural predators and parasites. Some species are much more susceptible than others, in particular the soft-leaved *Billbergia*, *Vriesea* and *Aechmea* species.

Above: Clusters of white scale form on the underside of leaves, the characteristic yellow spots from their feeding.

When the infestation is first noticed, control can sometimes be achieved by isolating the infested plants from healthy plants, as the bugs spread by means of little crawlers, which can only move a few metres unless blown by the wind. Scrape off the scale on the infected plants and wipe the leaves with a cotton swab lightly soaked in methylated spirits. This will help kill any eggs and crawlers that may have been left behind.

For an established infestation in a number of plants, chemicals will probably be needed. Use Applaud 25WP or Enstar II, following label rates for ornamentals; two applications spaced a fortnight apart should control this pest. This is an insect growth regulator which acts by preventing the insects from moulting, effectively suffocating them over time, and it is reasonably safe to use. Complete coverage of all leaf surfaces is necessary for satisfactory control.

A systemic alternative where complete coverage can't be guaranteed is powdered Orthene, which is very effective against scale and other insect pests, but must be applied with care due to its toxicity. Label rates for ornamentals can be used.

Slugs and snails
Large quantities of slugs and snails can be present in and around bromeliad plants and these can cause considerable damage to the flower stems and foliage, usually on the soft-leaved types, with *Pitcairnia* species particularly susceptible.

Slugs and snails are active throughout the year, but more so during periods of high humidity and moderately warm conditions such as spring and autumn. Snails have one breeding cycle per year, laying eggs in the spring, while slugs breed and lay eggs all year round if conditions are suitable. Snails are the predominant pest, so good control can be achieved with an intensive snail bait programme which is timed to coincide with the emergence of young snails in late spring.

Spider mites
Occasionally, red or spider mites may affect some of the soft-leaved *Vriesea* and *Guzmania*. This is reasonably rare, and is normally only a problem with indoor plants. The easiest way to control these pests is to increase humidity and spray the foliage frequently with water.

Spiders
Spiders can also be a problem, not because they do any damage to the plants, but rather from an aesthetic point of view as some spiders build webs over the plants, which can look unsightly. Personally, I prefer having the spiders, for all the good work they do in keeping other bugs under control.

Vase rot
The fungal disease *Phytophthora cinnamoni* is a common problem, and this can cause a vase rot, which is seen as a wet, dark blueish green or black rot of the base of inner leaves, usually starting in the white, soft portion of the leaf and a foul smell. Affected plants typically collapse and die before action can be taken, although if seen in time, the centre leaves and vase water should be removed immediately and then sprayed with a fungicide.

If this disease is suspected, there is a standard test developed by the pineapple industry which works for all bromeliads. Fill a glass jar with about 100 ml of water from a plant thought to be infected. Take a leaf from a healthy plant, and submerge the pale white end about 25 mm under the water. Incubate for about 7–10 days at

Above: Characteristic damage caused by copper toxicity from treated timber. This is now developing into fungal rot.

room temperature. If there is infection, it will show up as rot, with a line of blue-black tissue between the healthy and diseased areas. The rot will be foul smelling.

Phytophthora cinnamoni is a cosmopolitan disease which is present in most soils and free-standing water such as ponds, puddles and shallow bores, and is water borne and can move rapidly. The disease can often be found in potting mixes, particularly those which are based on young peat. It has a wide host range and infects nearly every plant family.

Damage to the newly emerging leaves in the vase can lead to *Phytophthora* infection. This may come about from salt burning from too much fertiliser in the cup, or chemical damage such as copper or oil sprays or drip from treated timber.

Fungal growth occurs mainly during warm, wet periods, so spring and autumn are the risky periods. If the disease is expected, use Aliette as a foliar spray every two weeks. This will assist in increasing a plant's resistance to infection; the label rates for ornamentals should be used. Phosphonic acid preparations such as Foli-R-Fos® or Foschek can also be effective as preventative sprays. For plants showing early signs of *Phytophthora*, tip out the vase

water, remove any rotten tissue and drench the plants with Ridomil® 10G. An alternative is Fongarid 25 WP which is also effective.

Weevils

A number of weevil species eat bromeliads; however, most of these are confined to their native lands and affect only limited numbers of plants. The notable exception is the weevil *Metamasius callizona*, native to southern Mexico and Central America, and which was discovered in mainland United States in 1989. It is now endangering Florida's rarest native bromeliads and, unfortunately, control methods for this weevil are very limited.

Other problems

A dry environment and lack of nutrients may also cause the browning or yellowing of leaf edges on any of the bromeliads. More water and feeding can fix this.

When green-leaved plants become tinged with red, typically on varieties of *Guzmania* and *Aechmea*, this is a sign of stress. It can be caused by low humidity and high light levels, particularly after pups have been planted out.

Bromeliads are particularly sensitive to high levels of some heavy metals. Excessive levels of copper, zinc and boron are all known to cause severe damage and will sometimes kill plants. Some species are much more sensitive than others, in particular most *Neoregelia*, *Aechmea*, *Guzmania*, *Billbergia* and the tank-forming tillandsias. In the early stages, heavy-metal damage is seen as a small brown spot on the lower part of the leaf, near where it joins the plant. This may only be the size of a small coin to start with but soon expands. It usually has a mushy appearance and is concentrated in the middle of the lower leaf, rather than the edges; over time this may actually rot out altogether, leaving a hole. If this leaf is removed, the next youngest leaf will also be seen to have the same mark. Eventually the whole plant will rot away at the base unless the source of heavy metals is removed.

It is important to remember never to plant bromeliads in greenhouses, shadehouses or conservatories constructed of timber treated with copper- or boron-based preservatives. Also, avoid planting under wooden decks or immediately adjacent to wooden fences. Some people have suggested that old treated timber is less likely to cause damage; however, some of the worst damage I have seen came from a greenhouse that had nearly 50-year-old treated timber in it. Painting the timber with several layers of acrylic paint seems to prevent most of the damage.

Never spray bromeliads with copper- or zinc-based pesticides; and avoid using water stored in galvanised or zinc-coated iron. Definitely avoid using rainwater caught by copper gutters or downpipes.

Bromeliads are also sensitive to many oil-based sprays, which block the important feeding and breathing scales on the leaves. Oils should never be used around bromeliads, unless a test is carried out first to check for safety — some people report that canola oil can be used safely, but again caution is needed.

Above: Although a very beautiful setting for bromeliads, this is in fact a toxic environment, as the copper leaching from the fountain will gradually kill any plants the water splashes on.

Above: Damage at the air/water interface of bromeliads is often caused by toxic products such as oil-based chemicals. In this case it was hot water from a hose left in the sun.

PROPAGATION

There are three ways of acquiring bromeliads for your garden: the most common starting point is a bromeliad donated happily by a friend or relative; soon you will start to notice bromeliads in your local garden centre, often tucked away in a corner; finally, when total addiction has set in, you must resort to other methods of increasing your collection, in other words propagating them yourself.

BUYING BROMELIADS

Although this may seem the simplest way of increasing your collection, there are a number of pitfalls which are peculiar to purchasing bromeliads from garden centres, florists, supermarkets and the like.

With the increasing popularity of bromeliads, there seems to be a mad scramble from growers to put plants on the market. Some of these plants are exceptional hybrids from top breeders, while others are tried and true varieties that have been around for years. Unfortunately though, there are many examples of garden centres selling plants that are underfed, damaged, diseased, and even old mother plants that have had their pups removed! Fortunately, with care the first three of these problems can be overcome, although sometimes it is only the pups that come right.

There are many traps for the unwary when buying bromeliads, and these mostly arise from buying plants that are not suited to the conditions where they will be planted. Unfortunately, many garden centres are still somewhat green when it comes to bromeliads — understandably, as it is a large family of relatively new and very diverse plants. A classic example are the very cold-sensitive varieties like *Aechmea chantinii*, *Guzmania* hybrids and *Vriesea* 'Splenriet' which are often sold as outdoor plants. These are great varieties, but as soon as night temperatures drop below 10°C, they will start to suffer and die so should only be purchased as indoor or hothouse plants unless you are in a truly tropical climate.

Poor labelling is another problem, with many bromeliads sold with very little cultural information and often the wrong name. This results in purchases which may be totally unsuited for the end situation. For example, the genus *Aechmea* contains both shade lovers and sun lovers, so if the plant is only described as an *Aechmea*, with no other information, the buyer would need to be quite experienced to work out if it will be best in the sun or shade.

Plants that have been flowered too young is another common problem. Nearly all commercial nurseries use a product which produces ethylene in the vase of the bromeliads to induce them to flower. Used correctly, this has no long-term effect on the plant. However, it is tempting for growers to induce flowering quickly, to increase turnover in the greenhouse, with the resulting problem being that the plants are often too small to support the large flower. As a result they will usually grow poorly, be more susceptible to disease and produce very few if any pups.

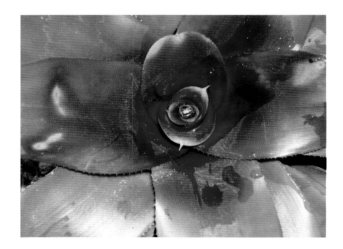

Above: The type of plant to avoid buying. This *Neoregelia* 'Debbie' has been dosed to flower too young, and will never develop the colour and intensity of a mature flowering plant. There is also some chemical burning from the treatment and calcium deposits from poor quality water supply.

How do you avoid these pitfalls? First of all, shop around. Look on the internet (there is a list of internet sites on page 195) and in books for information on varieties and their requirements. Many sites have photos, which can be used to compare for size and quality to those plants you are wanting to buy. Buy off people who know what they are talking about and are able to guide you. Check prices against online catalogues and mail order lists. Above all, please don't get disenchanted if you have fallen into the pitfalls above. Bromeliads are too good to ignore due to one bad experience.

One of the best ways to avoid many of these pitfalls is to buy bromeliads as offshoots. If kept in a cool, shady place with a misting of water every few days, pups will keep for weeks until you are ready to plant them. Pups can be difficult to purchase from normal retail outlets, but many smaller bromeliad nurseries will offer pups for sale and this is the most common way of buying them over the internet as well. Pups are usually sold for at least half the cost of buying fully grown plants, so this is the most economical way of building your collection. Pups are also much more suited to planting on trees, rocks or tree ferns as offshoots form new roots much quicker than flowering plants. In the garden, pups will acclimatise much faster and more easily than flowering plants. Once you obtain a source of pups from a good grower, you will probably never buy mature plants again.

SEED RAISING

Propagation from seed is the most common method used by commercial nurseries, but not home gardeners, which is a pity, as for many species, seed is relatively easy to germinate and is a low-cost way of quickly increasing a collection.

Seed can either be bought, and a good source is the seed banks of the various bromeliad societies, or collected from flowered plants. Seed must be collected when it has changed in colour from cream to dark brown, as immature seed will germinate poorly. Bromeliad seed must be sown fresh, as it quickly loses its viability, and seed that is too old is the most common cause of failure to germinate. Once the seed has been collected, it can be stored for short

Above: Two stages of berry colour in *Aechmea lueddemanniana* 'Rubra'. The white berries are yet to ripen to the deep purple.

periods in envelopes.

There are several types of seed produced by different species and each one is distributed differently. Sometimes the seed is held in little berries (*Aechmea*, *Neoregelia* and *Nidularium*, for example). These types are spread by birds and small animals that eat and excrete them. In other species the seeds are enclosed in capsules and attached to little 'parachutes' (*Vriesea* and *Tillandsia*, for example). These types are spread long distances by wind. A third type are the winged seeds (*Puya* species, for example) which are spread short distances by wind.

If you want to collect seed for propagation yourself, it is best to follow these methods. Genera that produce berries should be squeezed to release their seed, then washed over a fine gauze until clean. Lay the seed out on fine gauze trays to dry. Genera that produce air-blown seed should be harvested when the seed cases are just beginning to split. Lay these seed cases out in closed boxes or paper bags, where they can split and release the seed without losses.

Before sowing the seed, sterilise all the materials you will use for propagation, including trays, media, plastic bags and mesh, by soaking them in water at 70°C or more for at least half an hour. This will kill any fungi and bacteria which could cause many losses.

Sow seed of most varieties on the surface of wet sphagnum moss in propagating trays. Surface sowing is essential, as bromeliad seed needs some light to germinate. Fill the trays to within 2 cm of the top with sphagnum moss, sow the seed and then place cling film, glass or frost cloth over the tray and hold tight with a rubber band. If using cling film, prick several holes in the film to allow air movement. If you are using either glass or cling film, do not put the trays in direct sunlight, as the heat can build up rapidly and be devastating to the germinating seed.

Strongly epiphytic bromeliads such as many *Tillandsia* and *Vriesea* species can be sown on gauze mesh placed directly over a wet pad of cloth, to maintain high humidity at all times. A good alternative for these is to scatter them over tree fern slabs, where they germinate and grow well.

Bromeliad seed require frequent irrigation, even when covered by plastic. Typically 1–2 waterings per week will be needed for seed propagated on sphagnum moss. Irrigate by placing each tray in cool boiled water or by misting with a fine spray. Seed sown on mesh will germinate best when misted at least twice a day.

Bromeliad seed germinates best in temperatures of 22–24°C (although a range of 21–27°C is satisfactory), a relative humidity of 80–90% and a fairly low light level (no more than 18 klux for those with a light meter). Commercial nurseries use a climate-controlled room, specially designed for bromeliad seed germination to achieve ideal conditions. For the home gardener, this can be duplicated cheaply by using a heat pad in a well-lit room or small greenhouse and misting the seedlings each day.

Germination occurs within 2–3 weeks with *Guzmania*, *Tillandsia* and *Vriesea*. Planting out is done 5–6 months after sowing. Germination occurs within 1–2 weeks with *Aechmea*, *Billbergia*, *Nidularium* and *Neoregelia*. Planting out is done 2–3 months after sowing.

GROWING ON

Once the seed has germinated, the real work begins. It can take 2–15 years to produce a mature plant, depending on the species. Fast-growing plants such as *Aechmea gamosepala* can be pricked out into cell trays or very small (5 cm) pots within three months of germination, but slow species such as *Vriesea hieroglyphica* can take 12 months before they are big enough to prick out (at only 1 cm high!). During this time, many are lost through disease, insects and algae

Below: These *Vriesea* seedlings are less than 2 mm long despite being more than six months old.
Below right: *Nidularium* seedlings ready to be potted up.

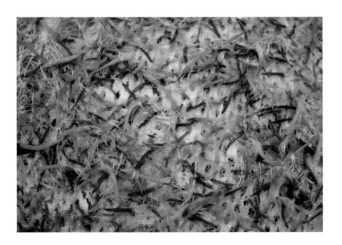

growth. It is not unusual to lose 50 percent of a line of plants between germination and pricking out. This high attrition rate is the reason that some bromeliads are so expensive to purchase. Compared to other plants, bromeliads are also generally very slow to grow from seed. However, as offshoot production is so slow for commercial bulking up, seed sowing is still the best method for a commercial nursery. In the Netherlands and Belgium, many millions of bromeliads are raised this way by specialist nurseries each year for the European market.

Once they are pricked out, the plants can be moved into another area, where climate is still partially controlled. For a home gardener, this may be a sun room, or a window facing the morning sun or a small greenhouse. The young plants can stay in this environment for another 3–9 months, depending on the species.

Once they have formed a good root system and some substantial leaves, by which time they may already be 6–21 months old, depending on the species, the plants can be potted up. They are still usually only 2–5 cm high, but are big enough to handle greenhouse conditions. They need to be placed in the correct light level for their species at this stage: low-light plants go under 50% shadecloth, partial-shade lovers under 20–30% shadecloth and full-sun lovers under 0–10% shade.

From there it can take 1–8 years to produce a mature plant, depending on the species.

OFFSHOOTS

Propagation by means of offshoots, commonly called pups by bromeliad lovers, is one of the most well-known characteristics of bromeliads. Many bromeliad fanciers started out their collection with a gifted bromeliad pup from a family member or friend. Apart from the pleasure received in starting a new bromeliad gardener off, or just the pleasure of simply propagating new plants so easily, it is actually beneficial to remove the pups as it encourages them to produce more. Also, in a garden situation bromeliads can easily become overgrown and messy. To prevent this, it is a good idea to work through each clump on a regular basis, say every spring and autumn, removing dead mother plants and excess pups. Often this can be done with the clump still in place; however, sometimes it is easier to lift the clump, divide it vigorously and replant.

Most, but not all species of bromeliads produce pups. Usually they are produced near or after flowering, after which time the plant (called the mother plant) usually dies. This can take 1–3 years, depending on the species and how well it was grown. From the time the mother plant starts flowering, to when it finally dies, it may produce 1–10 pups with most species producing 3–5 pups. There are a few species, fortunately not many, which don't pup at all, and these must be propagated from seed.

Pups can be left on or removed, depending on circumstances and personal preference. If they are left on, less pups will be produced and the mother plant will die earlier, but the pups will mature and flower more quickly. If they are removed, they will take longer to mature and flower, but more pups will be produced. Sometimes, some species look better as a clump; in other cases, a single plant is more dramatic.

On close inspection of the plants, it is obvious that different bromeliad species have quite different pupping habits. Most tank-forming bromeliads set new pups at the base of the mother plant, just below the lowest leaves, and these are probably the easiest to propagate.

However, some of the tank-types produce their pups within the plant, at any point from the base to near the top and these pups can be difficult to remove. Examples of these are *Vriesea hieroglyphica*, *V. zamorensis* and *Guzmania sanguinea*. The latter two typically produce only one pup that is so hard to remove that in practice it is almost never done; instead the pup is left to gradually grow through and take over the mother plant. It is very easy to remove pups from some of the species that produce pups this way. Various *Cryptanthus* for example have pups which almost fall off when touched.

Other bromeliads, such as *Neoregelia ampullacea*, *Billbergia amoena* 'Red', *Cryptanthus* 'Cascade', *Pitcairnia xanthocalyx* and *Bromelia balansae* produce a proportion of their pups on long stolons (otherwise called suckers). In the case of *B. balansae* and *P. xanthocalyx* these suckers grow under the ground. These stolons are quite useful for the plants: with the underground suckers, large areas can be

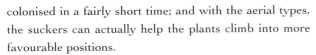

Above: *Cryptanthus* 'Cascade' showing its long stolons.
Right: A small plant of *Alcantarea imperialis*, already producing a multitude of grass pups.

colonised in a fairly short time; and with the aerial types, the suckers can actually help the plants climb into more favourable positions.

A few bromeliads have a tendency to produce what is known as 'grass pups'. These are very small pups which arise from the base of the plant, usually before flowering has occurred. They can be removed at this small stage and grown on just as you would a seedling. They may take some time to get established, but species that produce grass pups often do so in large numbers. Examples are *Tillandsia viridiflora*, *Alcantarea imperialis* and *Vriesea glutinosa*.

There are a few bromeliads, such as *Tillandsia secunda*, which produce pups on the flower stem, resulting in 30 or more pups. These are very easy to remove and grow on.

Pups that grow on stolons are the easiest to propagate, as they can simply be snapped or snipped off and transplanted. Sometimes the stolons are so long as to be a nuisance, and in these cases, just shorten them with secateurs. Pups that develop from the base are also usually fairly easy, as they come away with a sideways and downwards pull. Some of these pups are difficult to break off though and are best removed by cutting with secateurs or a sharp serrated knife.

Pups that develop in the leaves are usually much harder to remove without breaking them and often need a sharp serrated knife to separate from the mother plant. In this case it is usually better to remove the leaf immediately below the pup to get better access, then place the point of the knife at the join where the pup meets the mother plant and cut downwards.

I prefer removing pups by hand where possible, as the natural break zone is much less likely to rot than the cut left by a knife or secateurs. However, many people will find removing pups by hand to be too strenuous and the chances of snapping the pup off too high is also increased. Even some of the apparently easy plants to propagate, such as *Aechmea kertesziae*, can occasionally involve considerable grunting and cursing before the pup comes away.

The point at which the pup comes away is actually very important. With bromeliads, all the roots and new growth come from a very small zone on the plant, often less than 1 cm long. If you look carefully at a pup, for example *Aechmea gamosepala*, in most cases you will see that there is an elbow bend just above the point where it attaches to the mother plant. Below this point is the stolon, which may be virtually nonexistent in some species, such as *Vriesea platynema*. In other plants such as *Canistropsis billbergioides* it will be quite long. This part of the pup serves no significant purpose once the pup is removed and can be cut off if it is in the way. The heel itself is typically where most of the new roots will come from, and many pups will already have their first roots appearing from this area. Above this point is the growing point of the plant, where the new leaves and eventually the flower stem will be formed. If the pup is broken at this point, the break will be seen as a moist, white area, and a break here will usually result in the loss of the pup. However, some people have had success in applying rooting hormone to this break, healing it for a few days and then planting — worth trying if it is a valuable plant.

Remove young plants when they are at least a third to half the size of the original plant. Plants removed too small will take longer to set a root system and will grow slower initially. Pups removed later may not produce a sufficient root system before they flower.

Depending on the species and whether the pup is removed, it takes 1–5 years for a pup to produce a mature plant. The pup can be planted straight into the new

Below left: Two pups ready to be taken off this *Nidularium innocentii* var. *striatum*. Below: Remove the leaf immediately below the pups, by pulling sideways and out.
Bottom left: Now the pup can easily be pulled away using the same motion. Bottom right: Both pups show the characteristic 'heel' near the base. They should be planted 1–2 cm above this point.

location, unless it has a fleshy base (as do many of the larger *Vriesea* species), or it has been removed with a knife or secateurs, in which case it is better to dry the pup off for a week in a cool dark place to help prevent rotting. One of the amazing things about bromeliads is that the offshoots can happily survive for many months if given the occasional water. However, for best results, planting should be carried out in the week that plants are propagated.

Pups can be plunged into the potting mix or garden soil to about 1–3 cm above where leaves meet at the plant base. Planting too deeply may increase the risk of rot, and planting too shallow will result in unstable plants which may need support. If a pup does need support, the easiest way is to plunge three small stakes into the ground around the plant. If these are tucked between the leaves, very little movement should occur.

The best time to take pups and plant them is spring and autumn, when light levels and temperature assist the development of a good root system. Plant growth is at its most vigorous at this time of year. In summer, extra shade may be needed to prevent leaf scorch until the plants are established, and the added stress at this time of year from the intense light and dry conditions may cause the plant to suffer before it can set up its new root system. Of course, with epiphytic *Tillandsia* species, summer propagation is just as good as any other time, as their root systems are not needed for sustenance.

Winter is generally not a good time to remove pups, unless sufficient heat is supplied by means of a heated greenhouse, bottom heat from a heatpad or the garden is in a subtropical zone. Plants removed in winter are most likely to sulk and may rot away at the base before the root system can establish. Also, experience has shown that pups attached to their mother plant are much less likely to become damaged during cold weather, even when the mother plant suffers. This is probably partially due to the overhead protection given by the mother plant, but may also be due to the plant transferring as much of its resources as possible to the younger plants in an effort to keep them going.

Finally, a special case should be made for the pineapple. This is a great way to introduce children to the fascination of bromeliads and plants in general. Buy a pineapple from your greengrocer or supermarket, making sure it has a healthy crown of leaves — if these are turning yellow it may be about to die. Do not cut the top off! Rather, remove it by 'unscrewing' it from the pineapple. This is much fun to do for small children and has the benefit of leaving behind any pineapple flesh which will otherwise cause rotting. Now strip off the small lower leaves until about 1 cm of the stem is exposed. This is where the new roots will come from. Set the plant aside in a cool room for about one week, to allow it to heal.

Plant in free-draining potting mix in a pot the same diameter as the foliage, water well and place the plant in dappled light in a very warm spot. After a month or so, a root system should have formed and the pineapple plant can be potted up or planted out. It will need lots of room, plenty of water and a good amount of fertiliser and warmth to fruit.

BROMELIAD SOCIETY WEBSITES

The easiest way of locating bromeliad groups in your area is via their websites. From these, you can follow the numerous links to groups closer to you. Some websites are:

Brazilian Bromeliad Society: www.bromelia.org.br
Bromeliad Society International: www.bsi.org
Central Coast NSW Bromeliad Society:
broms.vinetex.com.au
Exotica Nursery and Garden Centre:
www.bromeliads.co.nz
Florida Council of Bromeliad Societies: www.fcbs.org

CONVERSION CHARTS

Centimetres	Inches
1	0.39
5	1.95
10	3.90
20	7.80
30	11.7

Metres	Feet
0.5	1.64
1.0	3.28
1.5	4.92
2.0	6.56

Celsius	Fahrenheit
0 C	32.0 F
1 C	33.8 F
2 C	35.6 F
3 C	37.4 F
4 C	39.2 F
5 C	41.0 F
6 C	42.8 F
7 C	44.6 F
8 C	46.4 F
9 C	48.2 F
10 C	50.0 F

Celsius	Fahrenheit
11 C	51.8 F
12 C	53.6 F
13 C	55.4 F
14 C	57.2 F
15 C	59.0 F
16 C	60.8 F
17 C	62.6 F
18 C	64.4 F
19 C	66.2 F
20 C	68.0 F

Celsius	Fahrenheit
21 C	69.8 F
22 C	71.6 F
23 C	73.4 F
24 C	75.2 F
25 C	77.0 F
26 C	78.8 F
27 C	80.6 F
28 C	82.4 F
29 C	84.2 F
30 C	86.0 F

INDEX

Page numbers in **bold** refer to illustrations